North Korea at
a Crossroads

North Korea at a Crossroads

Suk Hi Kim

McFarland & Company, Inc., Publishers
Jefferson, North Carolina, and London

LIBRARY OF CONGRESS CATALOGUING-IN-PUBLICATION DATA

Kim, Suk Hi, 1937–
  North Korea at a crossroads / Suk Hi Kim.
    p.   cm.
  Includes bibliographical references and index.

  ISBN 0-7864-1741-2 (softcover : 50# alkaline paper) ∞

  1. Korea (North)—History.   I. Title.
  DS935.K558   2003
  951.93—dc21   2003014572

British Library cataloguing data are available

On the front cover: top: Kim Il Sung; *bottom:* Kim Jong Il; *background:* ©2003 PhotoDisc

Manufactured in the United States of America

*McFarland & Company, Inc., Publishers
  Box 611, Jefferson, North Carolina 28640
  www.mcfarlandpub.com*

Acknowledgments

Many individuals have provided constructive advice critical to the development of *North Korea at a Crossroads*. First of all, my special thanks go to Dean Bahman Mirshab and Academic Vice President Gerald Stockhausen, S.J., who gave me a research leave in 2003 for this project.

I offer my thanks to American friends who provided detailed suggestions for this book: Stacey Banks (Clearly University), Rhonda DeLong (Eastern Michigan University), Kenneth Kim (SUNY at Buffalo), Richard Kowalczyk (University of Detroit Mercy), and John and Janet Sung (Windsong Radiology).

I gratefully acknowledge valuable comments and suggestions from my friends in Korea: Chang Dae Hwan (Meil Business Newspaper), Chang Soo Huh (LG Group), Kim Jay Kown (Words of life), Kim Hwang Joe (Yonsei University), and Park Yong Shuk (Yonsei University). I am especially grateful to Hyung Suk Kim (Korean Foundation for World Aid) and Thomas Park (Wayne State University School of Medicine) for their contribution of the article "The North Korean Famine and Korean NGOs," which serves as Chapter 8 of this book.

I am also grateful to my graduate fellows—Eun Young Choi and Yalda Ghorashyzadeh—for developing an instructor's manual

to complement this book, available online at www.mich.com/~ki.
suk.

Finally and importantly, Kim Jin Sun (my niece), Lee S(
Jung (Korean Foundation for World Aid), and Choi Yoon W(
(Korean Foundation for World Aid) deserve special acknowledg
ment for their contributions of information, translation, and sup
port.

Contents

Acknowledgments   v

Preface   1

Part I. Introduction

1. North Korea: Yesterday, Today, and Tomorrow   7

Part II. North Korea at a Crossroads

2. The Korean War (1950–1953):
   Causes and Consequences   37

3. North Korea's Continuing Survival:
   The Pathway of Confucianism and Self-reliance   51

4. Roads to Korean Unification   61

Part III. The North Korean
Economy and Its Open Door Policy

5. The North Korean Economy   77

6. Inter-Korean Economic Relations   99

CONTENTS

7. Doing Business with North Korea 115

8. The North Korean Famine and Korean NGOs 135
   by Hyung Suk Kim and Thomas T. Park

**Part IV. The Case for
Reconciliation with North Korea**

9. Eight Compelling Reasons for a Policy
   of Reconciliation with North Korea 153

Appendix A: Chronologies 179
Appendix B: Think Tanks for Korean Studies 193
Index 217

Preface

Many positive changes took place in the Korean peninsula from 1994 to 2000: the Agreed Framework of 1994 to abandon North Korea's nuclear ambitions in exchange for economic aid; a sunshine policy of engagement adopted in 1998 by South Korea with the endorsement of the United States; and the first ever summit of North and South Korean leaders in June 2000 after the establishment of two separate governments in 1948, to name a few. Relations between the U.S. and North Korea reached a high point in the final months of the Clinton administration. That trend culminated in a visit to Pyongyang by then Secretary of State Madeleine Albright, the highest-level U.S. official to travel to the North. Her visit came just a few weeks after a top North Korean official visited President Clinton in the White House in October 2000.

However, these improvements ended when President George W. Bush, inaugurated in January 2001, made known his intention to revert to a tougher line on relations with North Korea. In the past, the U.S. State Department had labeled North Korea, Iraq, and Iran "rogue states" whose military policy and support of other groups threatened Washington's security. In his State of the Union address on January 29, 2002, Bush called these three countries an "axis of evil." A series of hard-line moves taken by the U.S. and North Korea since then has caused their relationship to deteriorate. Consequently, daily headlines about this newly strained relationship between the two old enemies have filled the media around the world.

This current international crisis will eventually be resolved peacefully through dialogue because North Korea holds South Korea, Japan, and tens of thousands of U.S. troops hostage. Moreover, North Korea has maneuvering room in foreign policy because the five governments that must contend most directly with Pyongyang—Seoul, Washington, Beijing, Tokyo, and Moscow—do not want an abrupt shift in the status quo. However, North Korea will remain one of the global trouble spots as long as it exists as an independent communist state.

This book, *North Korea at a Crossroads,* examines past (e.g., the Korean War), current (e.g., the North Korean famine), and future (e.g., Korean unification) issues with North Korea.

COMMON FORMAT

Although there is some minor variation, each chapter of *North Korea at a Crossroads* follows more or less the same format:

At the beginning of each chapter, a summary gives an overview of the chapter, its importance, and the content of major sections.

The main text of each chapter integrates real world illustrations, key statistics, and policy options to clarify discussions of past, current, and future issues with North Korea.

In most chapters, a short conclusion provides readers with key points of the chapter for review.

A list of key terms and concepts is provided at the end of each chapter so that readers may test their comprehension and retention.

A section of questions supports book discussions. The questions reemphasize policy options, concepts, and implications.

A list of references concludes each chapter, leading readers to sources of additional information about specific topics discussed in the chapter.

Appendices at the end of the book offer timelines of Korean history (Appendix A) and addresses for think tanks in Korean Studies (Appendix B).

COMPLEMENTARY MATERIALS

An instructor's manual to complement this text is available on-line.

Each chapter in the instructor's manual includes chapter objectives, key terms, and concepts with definitions, a detailed summary that will provide readers with a handy overview of key concepts for review, and answers to end-of-chapter questions. See www.mich. com/~kimsuk for the instructor's manual and other useful information about this book.

PART I

Introduction

Part I, a single chapter, presents an overview of this book. The chapter covers the period from the division of Korea in 1948 to the future of North Korea beyond 2003, addressing a range of past, present, and future issues.

1 North Korea: Yesterday, Today, and Tomorrow

SUMMARY

The September 11, 2001, terrorist attacks against the World Trade Center in New York and the Pentagon in Washington, D.C., temporarily shifted America's attention from global trouble spots such as North Korea to Afghanistan. Now that the reign of the Taliban is over, the United States questions how to confront other states sponsoring terrorism and developing weapons of mass destruction. Policy makers face two choices: engagement and confrontation. In the past, the Clinton administration had engaged with North Korea to prevent its development of nuclear, chemical, and biological weapons. The Bush administration quickly put North Korean relations on hold until a policy review was conducted. By early July 2001, the new administration's policy, under the influence of Colin Powell, validated a continuation of the U.S.–North Korean dialogue. However, North Korea expressed its strong concern through other channels that the Bush administration operated under a different and more difficult set of principles than the Clinton administration. North Korea's concern was validated on January 29, 2002, when Bush in his state of the union address labeled Iran, Iraq, and North Korea an "axis of evil," stating that he would focus on them as he extended his war on terrorism. Since then the relationship between the United States and North Korea has deteriorated from engagement to containment; from containment to confrontation; and from confrontation to crisis—first regional, then international. This chapter examines that progression and considers the issues between the two nations—past, present and future.

Introduction

Given the gravity and urgency of North Korean issues, it is important for the U.S. to address highly uncertain prospects in the North. Although Korea is a middle-size country—North and South Korea together are roughly the same size as Britain and have a combined population of 70 million—Koreans feel small, because they live amid giants. Their geopolitical neighbors are China, Japan, Russia, and America whose spheres of influence overlap in Korea. As a result, the peninsula has been the site over the past 50 years of recurrent collisions between great-power interests. Nevertheless, recent events in the Korean peninsula—the death of Kim Il Sung who had ruled North Korea for 45 years, the rise of his eldest son Kim Jong Il as the new leader of the North, a North Korean famine in the 1990s, the U.S. treatment of North Korea as a terrorist sponsor, the development of nuclear weapons by North Korea, the rise of South Korea as a newly industrialized country, and its financial crisis of 1997—have generated new attention on Korea as one of the global trouble spots.

Ever since the Korean War, two rival governments, the communist in the North and the capitalist in the South, have been locked in mortal combat. Half a century later, there is still no peace on the horizon. By American estimates, North Korea has 1.1 million troops; South Korea has 700,000, which are augmented by 37,000 Americans in a combined force structure. All men have military experience, and millions (the number of reserve troops is 4.7 million in North Korea and 4.5 million in South Korea) are eligible for call-up in case of war (Ratnsear, 2003). Since Kim Il Sung died of a heart attack on July 8, 1994, the future of North Korea became the core of Northeast Asian security issues. Arguments focus on North Korea's current situation, its policy directions, and the results of its policies.

The history of contention between North and South dates from World War II, when the Japanese emperor accepted the Allies' ultimatum of unconditional surrender on August 15, 1945. At the end of World War II, the U.S. and the Soviet Union agreed that U.S. forces would occupy South Korea and Soviet troops would occupy North Korea to disarm Japanese troops. This occupation was intended to be a temporary arrangement until elections supervised by the United Nations (UN) would be held to form one government for Korea. The U.S.-Soviet Joint Commission held a series of meetings in 1946 and 1947, but failed to reach any agreement. Then in September 1947, the UN General Assembly adopted a resolution to hold general elections in Korea to insure immediate independence and unification. However, the Soviet Union and their communist followers in the North refused to comply with the UN resolution and obstructed the entry of the UN Commission on Korea (UNCK) into North Korea.

In order to accomplish its mission in Korea, the UNCK carried out national elections on the peninsula south of the 38th parallel on May 10, 1948. On August 15, 1948, the government of the Republic of Korea was officially proclaimed and Syngman Rhee took the oath of office as the first president of the Republic of Korea. Without the UN involvement, the North Korean communists held their own elections in September 1948 and under the tutelage of Russia, Kim Il Sung established the so-called Democratic People's Republic of Korea. Thus, the 38th parallel became the Berlin Wall of Korea.

Some fifty years later, after Korea was divided south and north of the 38th parallel, South Korea has defeated North Korea economically. The only question remaining is whether victory will eventually eradicate North Korea or prompt it to reconstruct itself as a modern state compatible with the economic and strategic realities of Northeast Asia. South Korea, the U.S., China, Japan, and

Russia will have to decide what Korean unification means and thus maneuver to preserve the current partition or attempt to push the North into unification with the South. We attempt to address this important question by examining past, current, and future issues with North Korea.

THE KOREAN WAR (1950–1953)

On January 12, 1950, Dean Acheson, the U.S. Secretary of State, disclosed in a speech at the National Press Club in Washington, D.C., that South Korea was outside the U.S. defense perimeter. His speech was viewed as a green light by the North Korean communists to cross the 38th parallel. On the morning of June 25, 1950, North Korea attacked South Korea, captured the South Korean capital of Seoul within four days, and subsequently overran two-thirds of South Korea within a short period of time. Five days after the North Korean invasion, President Harry S Truman sent American air and naval forces to assist South Korea. A few days later, he authorized the bombing of specific targets in North Korea, approved the use of ground forces in the fighting, and started a naval blockade of the entire Korean coast.

Both South Korean and U.S. forces took a last stand in the Pusan region in the southeastern corner of the peninsula. Realizing the grave danger to South Korea's existence, Truman requested the assistance of UN members. Consequently, troops from 15 other countries joined the South Korean and U.S. forces in the fight against North Korea. On September 15, 1950, UN forces made a successful amphibious assault far behind North Korean lines at Inchon and conquered its forces in the South. The UN forces recaptured Seoul on September 28 and captured the North Korean capital of Pyongyang on October 19, 1950.

To prevent the defeat of North Korea, however, 150,000 Chinese troops poured into Korea in the middle of October and pushed the UN forces back to the 38th parallel. Inconclusive but fierce fighting continued for two years while truce negotiations were being held. An armistice agreement (July 27, 1953) between the warring parties ended three years of fighting and established a demilitarized zone near the original border at the 38th parallel. North and South Korea, however, remain in a technical state of war because later negotiations for a peace treaty between the two nations failed. To this date, a Military Armistice Commission (MAC) and a Neutral Nations Supervisory Commission (NSC) continue to supervise the truce. The MAC is composed of five officers from North and South Korea to supervise the armistice and settle any violations through negotiations. The NSC consists of officers from Sweden, Switzerland, Poland, and Czechoslovakia, who carry out specific functions of supervision, observation, inspection, and investigation.

North Korea's ambition to conquer South Korea by force fortunately failed, but the war caused enormous property damage and over 1.6 million combat casualties. Nearly 147,000 South Korean forces and 35,000 UN soldiers died during the bitter three-year war. North Korean and Chinese forces suffered approximately 1.42 million casualties over the same period (Korean Information Service, 1986). These figures, however, cannot convey the horrors the war inflicted on the Korean people. Even to this day, the South is concerned over possible military actions by the North.

After the end of the Korean War, the U.S. adopted a general policy of military containment, diplomatic isolation, and economic sanctions against North Korea. In order to prevent another war, Washington signed a mutual security treaty with Seoul in 1953. Furthermore, to implement its anticommunist containment policy in Asia, the U.S. signed a series of bilateral and multilateral security treaties with South Korea, Japan, the Philippines, Thailand, and New Zealand. However, the U.S.-led coalition with Japan and Korea faced a counter-alliance between North Korea, the Soviet Union and China. In the 30-year Treaty of Friendship, Alliance, and Mutual Assistance signed in February 1950, the Soviet Union and China agreed to use "necessary means" to prevent the revival of Japanese imperialism. This Sino-Soviet treaty served as a model for North Korea's mutual defense treaties with the Soviet Union and China that were signed in 1961. These treaties by two rival camps fully integrated the Korean peninsula into the Cold War bipolar framework (Eberstadt and Ellings, 2001).

However, a series of events since the late 1980s transformed the relations among the two Koreas and four Pacific powers from confrontation to cooperation. The four Pacific powers—China, Japan, Russia, and the U.S.—significantly expanded the scope of their cooperation in military, diplomatic, and economic fields. South Korea increased the level of cooperation with these four powers during the same period. Even North Korea gradually improved its relations with South Korea, Japan, and the U.S. until President Bush labeled North Korea as an "axis of evil" in his State of the Union address on January 29, 2002. In other words, the axis-of-evil remark by Bush effectively stalled many reforms in North Korea and reversed the relations between North Korea and other countries from cooperation to confrontation.

JUCHE PRINCIPLE

Under the custodianship of Kim Il Sung and Kim Jong Il, *juche* (the principle of self-reliance) has guided North Korea's ideology. *Juche* is credited to Kim Il Sung, who is characterized in the 1998 socialist constitution and elsewhere as "a genius ideological theoretician." The first syllable, *ju*, means "the main or fundamental" principle; the second syllable, *che*, means body, self or the foundation of something. Kim introduced *juche* in a speech to the Korean Workers Party in an effort to agitate party workers on December 28, 1955, when he was still trying to eliminate his rival politicians. *Juche*, repeated endlessly in classrooms and in the media, emphasizes national self-reliance, independence, and worship of the supreme leader. Although North Koreans often fail to follow the teachings of *juche* in their everyday lives, the ideology remains a powerful influence on their domestic and international policies.

Kim Jong Il transformed *juche* from a nationalistic ruling ideology to a cult ideology. Kim Jong Il was officially introduced as

Kim Il Sung's successor in 1980. Not being a soldier, a statesman, or an economist, Kim Jong Il's role was to interpret and propagandize the *juche* ideology and oversee cultural affairs. Because he was accountable to no one except his father, Kim Jong Il made *juche* an article of faith rather than a guide to practice all matters (Oh and Hassig, 2000).

North Korea's economy prominently applies to the ideological principle of *juche* under the following three principles. First, the 1998 revision of the North Korea's constitution stipulates that all means of production are owned solely by the state and cooperative organizations. All industrial facilities and commercial enterprises are state owned. Most farms operate as collectives under the strict guidance of the party. Under the second economic principle of central planning, the state formulates unified and detailed plans to guarantee a high rate of production growth and balanced development of the national economy. The third economic principle of *juche* is self-sufficiency, that is to say, socialist production relations are based upon the foundation of independent national economy. In accordance with the *juche* principle, North Korea's foreign trade amounts only to around 10 percent of gross national product (GNP), far below that of most other economies.

Kim's speech also revealed a core concept of national self-reliance and pride. Thus, North Korea adapted Marxist-Leninist principles to Korean conditions, rather than accept them wholesale. However, the Western press ridiculed his appeal to nationalism because during the Korean War, China had saved North Korea as a state and the Soviet aid strove to rebuild its economy. Of course, other measures of its dependence, such as reliance on foreign powers for economic aid and military support, eroded the belief that the North is a self-reliant country. Consequently, the original idea of self-reliance underwent revisions in the intervening years to make it compatible with evolving interpretations of *juche*. It is not unusual in North Korea to revise original texts for later publication to make them consistent with more recent ideological thought. For North Koreans, *juche* is inseparable from socialism and is considered the only means by which the masses can gain independence. Still, whatever changes evolved in the *juche* concept over the years, North

Korea's commitment to socialism as an organizational principle has never changed.

As *juche* developed, the principle addressed several major issues. First, it served to maintain North Korea's independence in the international community. Second, it modeled the North Korean people into ever-loyal disciples of the leader, but at the same time it gave them an individual purpose as "masters of society." Third, it glorified the solidarity of the people as a modern Confucian family around the party and its leader. Fourth, it defended North Korea's brand of socialism in the face of declining living standards and the collapse of the international communist bloc. Finally, under increasingly miserable conditions in the wake of Kim Il Sung's death, it gave the people a reason to live, even to die, for the regime.

It seems that most people support the idea of *juche* as a principle of national sovereignty, pride, and self-sufficiency. Pride in one's own country and the desire to preserve its independence characterize all nations. National self-sufficiency appeals to everyone, but people with knowledge of economics realize that national economies must operate interdependently. However, North Korea has used *juche* to control the masses. *Juche* as a label has been attached to any idea promoted by the Kims. *Juche* farming, for example, prescribes when and how crops are to be planted; *juche* steel dictates the steelmaking process. In all cases, *juche* strives to make local production units self-sufficient as the nation progresses to self-sufficiency; *juche* ideology functions as an anchor to keep the North Korean state from moving with the times.

In the 1990s, the North Korean economy ground to a halt as its people faced disease and starvation, and communist countries elsewhere toppled like dominos. How in hard times like this did the North Korean masses accept or at least tolerate socialism, and the greatness of the leader who brought them to ruin? First, North Korea forced people to engage in endless study and self-criticism so that they would be loyal to the leader and the party indefinitely. Second, they have never experienced political or social freedom. During the Choson dynasty, many of them worked for landlords. Shortly after the turn of the century, the entire economy was geared to supply Japan. After World War II, the communists imposed a

14

centralized form of nonparticipatory government. To the North Korean people, life in this autocratic society was business as usual. Third, the masses in North Korea differ in an important respect from those in the former Soviet Union and Eastern Europe—they are cut off from outside information. Because North Koreans have little information about life or thought outside, they have nothing else to believe if they reject what they are told. Finally, even if they were not committed on some ideological points and disbelieved others, they had no energy to pursue their own thoughts and no opportunity to discuss them. So, to avoid complicating life, they abandoned political thought and resigned themselves to repeating the political lessons they were taught.

NORTH KOREA'S NUCLEAR WEAPONS PROGRAM

In 1989, it became undeniably obvious that North Korea was assembling the elements of a nuclear weapons program. However, North Korea's program of nuclear technology emerged as early as the late 1950s; it gained momentum in the 1960s and again in the mid–1980s. North Korea initially obtained a small research reactor from Russia and later began construction on a larger reactor at the Yongbyon site. U.S. intelligence discovered this reactor under construction in 1984 and pressured Moscow to gain North Korean agreement to the Nuclear Non-Proliferation Treaty (NPT) in late 1985. A series of delays kept the International Atomic Energy Agency (IAEA) inspectors away from Yongbyon for several years. In 1989, the U.S. Central Intelligence Agency obtained conclusive evidence of a North Korean reprocessing facility near the main reactor at Yongbyon.

The year 1991—the end of the cold war—inaugurated a new turn of events that are still unfolding; its culmination is still uncertain. In that year, both Russia and China moved toward a two-Korea policy, with obstacles to the South's joining the UN removed, thus forcing the long resistant North to accept dual membership.

Consequently, the two Koreas became members of the UN in 1991. Now, North Korea had even greater reason to seek normalization of relations with the U.S. and Japan. At the same time, the U.S. tried to develop relations with North Korea because it recognized that any outbreak of hostilities on the peninsula would constitute a serious blow to the region and its own economic security.

The U.S., however, stipulated that progress on U.S.–North Korean relations had to be tied to advances in inter–Korean talks and that North Korea had to permit the IAEA to inspect its nuclear facilities. By mid–1991, the North was prepared to move in these directions. The U.S. then withdrew its tactical nuclear weapons from South Korea in 1991. In January 1992, North Korea signed a nuclear safeguard agreement with the IAEA, which inspected its nuclear facilities six times between May 1992 and January 1993 (Swomley, 2002). In spite of this improvement in North-South relations, U.S. and South Korean forces conducted Team Sprit 1993 war exercises to harass North Korea. North Korea announced its intention to withdraw from the NPT in March 1994, shut down its 5-megawatt reactor to unload fuel rods in May 1994, and rejected IAEA inspections of its military sites, thereby provoking an international crisis.

As President Bill Clinton opted for military actions against North Korea in early June 1994, former President Jimmy Carter re-entered the Korea saga to play another historic role. At 69 years of age, Carter had already played a post-presidential intermediary role in the Middle East, Ethiopia, Sudan, Somalia, and the former Yugoslavia. His trip to Pyongyang on June 15, 1994, set the stage for resolving this crisis peacefully as North Korea agreed to freeze its nuclear program and permit the two remaining IAEA inspectors to remain in North Korea until the completion of the planned third round of U.S.–North Korea nuclear negotiations. In fact, his mission to North Korea saved President Clinton from the most catastrophic military crisis of his presidency. Jimmy Carter received a Nobel Peace Prize in 2002 in recognition of his contribution for world peace and charitable activities.

After a period of intense negotiations, the U.S. and North Korea reached the Agreed Framework in October 1994, which was

16

one consequence of engagement (Mazarr, 1998). Under this agreement, North Korea pledged to abandon its nuclear program ambitions and to remain in the NPT regime. In exchange, the U.S. agreed to offer North Korea two light water reactors (LWR), interim deliveries of oil, and expanded contacts with the U.S. and other powers. As a result, the Korean Energy Development Organization (KEDO) was born to construct the LWRs and to provide North Korea with 500,000 tons of fuel oil per year during the construction of the LWRs. This Agreed Framework created a mechanism for North Korea to interact in a constructive fashion with South Korea, the U.S., and other participants in the arrangement.

In spite of many disputes over details of this agreement, it had served its purpose of capping North Korea's nuclear weapons program. North Korea had complied with the letter of the framework law, shut down its main Yongbyon reactor and the reprocessing facility, allowed repeated IAEA site visits, and done everything else the agreement called for. At the same time, the KEDO program had gone forward, with groundbreaking ceremonies taking place on August 19, 1997. Completion of the project is scheduled for 2004, with an estimated cost of about $5 billion.

On August 31, 1998, North Korea sent a three-stage rocket roaring into the heavens from a launch site on the shores of the Sea of Japan, which both North and South Korea call "The East Sea." So far as U.S. monitors could determine, the effort to launch a satellite failed. However, the range of the rocket, especially the third stage, was the most unpleasant discovery for those concerned about North Korea's potential for launching ballistic missiles with highly lethal and destructive warheads. In mid–September 1999, North Korea agreed to a moratorium on further missile tests while talks continued. In return President Clinton lifted some sanctions that banned most U.S. exports to and imports from North Korea. However, it continues to develop a two-stage missile that would be capable of reaching parts of the western United States. Moreover, some analysts believe that North Korea is not only capable of developing many nuclear weapons but that the country already has one or two nuclear weapons that could be mounted on those missiles. Thus, the U.S. has used this kind of information to justify its plans for multi-billion-dollar missile defense systems capable of shooting down a limited ICBM attack on the U.S. In other words, U.S. officials insist that the missile defense program is to defeat strikes by North Korea and other "rogue" nations.

In April 1996, the U.S. and South Korea proposed the four-party talks—the U.S., North and South Korea, and China—to solve the pending issues between the two Koreas. This format was a compromise between the two extreme options suggested by North and South Korea. North Korea has tried to bypass Seoul through direct negotiations with Washington. South Korea, on the other hand, has insisted on talks between the primary parties on the Korean peninsula.

The four-party talks contain several advantages. First, they signal the beginning of a face-to-face dialogue among the parties to the Korean War directed at replacing the truce with a lasting structure for peace. Second, the talks provide an arena in which the U.S. and South Korea may use China as a lever against North Korea. Third, North Korea may see the talks as a vehicle with which to come closer to the U.S. Fourth, China can use this forum as a means to maintain good relations with the U.S. and other western powers for its own economic and security interests.

Though this four-party meeting seemed to have a high probability of success, these talks went nowhere. Until the second preliminary session, North Korea had reiterated its position that the agenda should include a permanent peace agreement between Pyongyang and Washington along with withdrawal of U.S. troops stationed in South Korea—precisely the items that the U.S. and South Korea were not prepared to concede. Only after food aid was promised for 1998 did North Korea agreed to attend the first formal meeting held in Geneva on December 9, 1999.

From October 3 to October 5, 2002, the U.S. and North Korea had their first high-level contact in Pyongyang after a nearly two-year hiatus, but they failed to reach any agreement on a range of security issues. In fact, this brief interaction effectively worsened U.S.–North Korean relations. North Korea charged that James Kelly, U.S. Assistant Secretary of State for East Asian and Pacific Affairs, visited North Korea not to negotiate but to make the following demands: the suspension of the nuclear weapons program, verifiable controls on missile production and exports, the reduction of conventional forces along the 38th parallel, and the improvement of human rights. To the Bush administration's surprise, North Koreans admitted to Kelly that his evidence about their secret nuclear weapons program was correct. The North's admission of these actions violates the 1994 Agreed Framework, in which it pledged to abandon its nuclear weapons program in return for the construction of two light-water reactors and 500,000 tons of fuel oil each year until the reactors were completed.

North Korea offered talks with the U.S. to rectify the concerns over its nuclear weapons program. However, the Bush administration rejected these proposals, which were actually similar to North Korea's repeated offers over the last 50 years to give up its nuclear weapons program in exchange for a nonaggression pact with the U.S. In addition, Japan, South Korea, and the European Union agreed that oil deliveries to North Korea should continue, as it represented the best available bait to lure the nation away from developing weapons of mass destruction. However, on November 14, 2002, the Executive Board of the KEDO decided to end their monthly fuel deliveries to North Korea under heavy pressure from the Bush administration. In late December 2002, North Korea evicted international nuclear inspectors in a move to restart its main nuclear weapon complex, which experts believe could produce several powerful nuclear weapons within months.

In 1968, Great Britain, the U.S., and the Soviet Union signed a Treaty on the Non-Proliferation of Nuclear Weapons, usually called the Non-Proliferation Treaty (NPT) to halt the spread of atomic weapons; the UN approved the treaty on March 5, 1970. Under the treaty, five permanent members of the UN Security Council—China, France, Great Britain, the Soviet Union, and the U.S.—agreed not to transfer nuclear weapons to other nations and not to assist other nations to develop their own nuclear devices. The IAEA, the UN watchdog that monitors the 1970 treaty, consists of 187 countries as signatories. Today only four other countries—Cuba, India, Israel, and Pakistan—are not signatories. South Korea joined the IAEA on April 23, 1975, while North Korea joined

PART I. INTRODUCTION

Table 1.1: Balance of Forces
for North and South Korea

Variable	North Korea	South Korea	United States
Gross national product	$22 billion	$865 billion	$10 trillion
Military budget	$5.12 billion	$11.8 billion	Not available
Active troops	1.1 million	0.686 million	37,140
Reserve troops	4.7 million	4.5 million	Not available
Battle tanks	3,500	2,300	259
Artillery	10,400	4,774	90
Submarines	26	20	0
Surface combat ships	3	39	0
Combat aircraft	621	555	159

Note: Gross national product is expresssed in purchasing power parity. U.S. figures (with an exception of its gross national product) represent U.S. forces in South Korea.

Sources: Romesh Ratnesar, "How Dangerous Is North Korea," *Time,* January 13, 2003, p. 24; and *The World Factbook*, the Central Intelligence Agency, the United States, *www.cia.gov*, February 23, 2003.

it on December 12, 1985. On January 10, 2003, North Korea pulled out of the IAEA on the ground that the U.S. continues to maintain its hostile policy toward the country.

The latest standoff between the U.S. and North Korea on nuclear weapons created a climate for the brink of another war on the Korean peninsula. The January 13, 2003, cover story of *Time* reported, "North Korea, though much poorer than South Korea, has a bigger army and is rapidly expanding its ballistic-missiles. Experts fear it could threaten the continental U.S. with a nuclear, chemical or biological missile by 2015." Table 1 shows the balance of forces for North and South Korea. North Korea has more manpower, armor, and artillery, but South Korea has a better-equipped navy, advanced technology, and a powerful friend in the U.S.

The End of the Cold War

In 1989 the Soviet Union relaxed its control over the eastern European countries that had suffered its domination for over 40 years. These countries immediately seized the opportunity to throw off authoritarian communist rule with the fall of the Berlin Wall in 1989. Two years later, the Soviet Union itself underwent a political and ideological upheaval, which quickly led to its breakup into 15 independent states. With the end of the Cold War, there is no longer a bipolar system that guarantees peace and stability in Northeast Asia. It is doubtful whether Russia will ever regain the international stature of its Cold War era. Japan and China are cautiously but definitely trying to shed the image of a secondary role. Complicating the calculus of power in post–Cold War Northeast Asia is that the two Koreas are still locked in a structure reminiscent of bipolar confrontation, even though they have made some gestures of rapprochement since the end of the Cold War.

In the meantime, North Korea was slipping badly on virtually every front. Pursuing autarkic economic policies, it increasingly separated itself from the scientific-technological revolution taking place elsewhere. Its economic structure, moreover, was skewed toward heavy industry and the needs of the huge military sector so that consumer goods were in short supply. By the end of the 1980s, the growth rate had slowed to a minimal level.

Shortly thereafter, a series of crises engulfed the North. The collapse of the Soviet Union and the political upheavals in East Europe had a serious effect upon the North Korean economy because most of North Korea's trade had been with the Soviet Union and East Europe. Flood damage in 1995 and 1996 accelerated a steep economic decline. Severe energy shortages caused key industrial plants to operate at less than 50 percent.

In the fall of 1995, North Korea asked for international economic assistance for the first time in history. The U.S., Japan, and South Korea responded with foot aid as did certain international agencies. China, moreover, emerged as a key source of help, giving oil and grain, some at "friendship prices" and some gratis.

THE SUNSHINE POLICY

South Korea's Kim Dae Jung government, inaugurated in February 1998, adopted a sunshine policy of engagement toward the North (Kim, 2000). The purpose of this policy was to legally allow individuals, organizations, and even the government to provide aid to North Korea in spite of the hostility of North Korea toward the government in Seoul. In other words, the sunshine policy is designed to separate humanitarian and business issues from political issues. This form of engagement was seen as the most promising choice for changing North Korea and reducing its threats. This sunshine policy is based on three principles: South Korea will not tolerate any armed provocation from the North; it will not seek to absorb North Korea; and it will make every effort to promote reconciliation and cooperation with the North.

At first, North Korea resisted. It publicly denounced the sunshine policy as a devious ploy to bring it down, an attempt to weaken its military readiness. In addition, this policy did not go well at the outset for at least two reasons. First, its inducements targeted both the government and the people of North Korea but not strongly enough to move either one. Second, the success of the policy relied too heavily on the willingness of the Kim Jong Il government to voluntarily change its policies. Unlike the previous governments of South Korea, however, President Kim encouraged the U.S., Japan, and other friends to engage in dialogue with North Korea and to give it economic assistance.

The U.S. and Japan publicly stated their strong support for the sunshine policy. Even traditional friends of North Korea such as China and Russia urged North Korea to engage in dialogue with the South. The turning point came on March 9, 2000, when President Kim announced the Berlin Declaration at the Berlin Free University in Germany. He reiterated the three principles of the sunshine policy. Kim stressed that his government did not want to realize unification by absorbing the North in the way German unification was brought about. South Korea does not have the ability or feel the necessity to do so. Finally, Kim proposed that the top leaders of the two sides hold a summit.

1. NORTH KOREA

The leaders of capitalist South Korea and communist North Korea met in Pyongyang on June 13, 2000, for the first time since the establishment of two separate governments in 1948, three years after Korea's liberation from Japanese colonial rule. The two leaders agreed in principle to reduce tension on the Korean peninsula and to increase economic, social, and cultural exchanges. Surprisingly, Kim Jong Il accepted an invitation to visit Seoul in 2001, but he did not fulfill his promise.

Many positive changes had taken place in North-South Korean relations since the historic June 2000 summit talks. The most visible outcome of the new policy has been North Korea's cooperation with Hyundai for the development of the Mt. Kumgang tourism project. Both sides also agreed to re-link the severed South-North railway and build a new highway to link the South to Kaesong City just north of the demilitarized zone. Other attempts, successful and unsuccessful, have been made to advance progress on such issues as divided family exchange reunions, the cancellation of U.S.-South Korean military exercises, economic assistance, drafts of agreements on investment protection, double taxation avoidance, and business dispute arbitration. President Kim Dae Jung received a Nobel Peace Prize in 2001 in recognition of the sunshine policy and other contributions.

Some analysts argue that North Korea has recently initiated a policy of internal reform and external engagement. In their view, the greatest contribution that the U.S. could make in order to achieve durable peace and stability on the Korean peninsula would be to normalize diplomatic relations with North Korea and enter into an extensive program of engagement. In other words, more extensive engagement with the North will create fissures within the North Korean policy and hasten desirable internal change.

THE NORTH KOREAN ECONOMY

In the first years after the Korean War, the centrally directed economy of North Korea had grown more rapidly than the more loosely controlled economy of South Korea. North Korea opted for an inner-directed economy, centered on building its heavy industry at home and shying away from commitments abroad. Part of the reason for an economic success of such a policy was that North Korea emphasized mass mobilization and used non-economic incentives to spur workers—these proved very effective in the early years. However, in the absence of rational economic inputs, these advantages soon reached their limits. Early economic success also owed much to massive economic aid and technical help from China and Russia (Christenson, 2000).

Predictably, the North Korean economy began to contract as the collapse of the socialist bloc in 1990 deprived North Korea of major markets. Because North Korea issues no consistent macroeconomic statistics, it is impossible to know the accurate picture of its economy. Nevertheless, the Bank of Korea estimates that the gross national product (GNP) of North Korea fell from $23.1 billion in 1990 to 12.6 billion in 1998 or by 55 percent. Its foreign trade declined by 70 percent in the same period as the country's economy contracted and trade relations with the former communist countries dwindled.

In 1998, the country's foreign debt, in default since the 1980s, amounted to $12 billion, not a large figure for most countries, but equaling 96 percent of this country's GNP. North Korean factories are estimated to have operated at no more than 25 percent of capacity in the 1990s (Oh and Hassig, 2000). The health care system virtually ceased to operate; a food shortage became a pressing economic problem. As a result, the number of premature deaths had ranged from 1,000,000 to 3,000,000 in the 1990s (Oh and Hassig, 1999).

Why did North Korea suffer from negative economic growth for almost ten years? Although many explanations have been offered for this decline, its economic slowdown began with the collapse of the international cooperation network among socialist countries. Four reasons stand out: increase of import prices, demand decline through market contraction, changes in the payment system, and capital withdrawal by Russia and China. First, the destruction of the cooperative system among socialist countries abolished socialist friendly prices, which usually ranged between one-fourth to one-third of regular market prices. Second, the breakdown of the cooperative network among socialist countries resulted in market contraction and a decrease in demand. Third, the payment system changed from a quasi-barter system to a payment system with hard currencies. Finally, in the late 1980s, China and Russia stopped providing new loans and began to demand the repayment of outstanding loans. Consequently, North Korea now suffers from shortages of foreign currency, grain, spare parts, oil, low international competitiveness, morale, and weak technology; and poor product quality, living standards, and production facilities.

While enjoying economic benefits from South Korean business firms, the North Korean economy finally turned around in 1999. The Bank of Korea estimates that the North Korean economy grew by 6.2 percent in 1999, 1.3 percent in 2000, 3.7 percent in 2001, and 1.2 percent in 2002, after experiencing nine years of successive negative growth. In particular, North Korean grain output recorded gains and its import volume expanded rapidly during the last few years. In addition, the average operation ratio of several industrial facilities of North Korea increased from 46 percent in February 1997 to 77 percent in 2001 (Lee, 2002)

The North Korean economy has turned around since 1999 for several reasons. The Hyundai Group of South Korea has paid somewhere between $150 to $200 million per year for the Mt. Kumgang tourism project. China and Russia have increased their economic assistance to North Korea. Humanitarian assistance from the U.S., Japan and other countries has increased as well. In addition to this external help, North Korea has initiated several new measures in recent years. Since 1998, for example, the announced goal of North Korea has been to build a national wealth. In order to achieve this goal, North Korea has emphasized two major areas: normalization of its leading industries and the improvement of living standards for its people. All of these factors have contributed to North Korea's economic growth in the past few years. North Korea, however, does not have sufficient production capacity to accommodate domestic consumption and to compensate for capital depreciation. Consequently, the recent positive economic growth in North Korea is vulnerable and could evaporate at any time.

This crisis forced North Korea to think seriously about the future of its autarkic system, resulting in a host of new laws on foreign investment, relations with capitalist firms, and new zones of free trade. North Korea recently promulgated many banking, labor, and investment laws. It could reap numerous benefits from its expanded economic cooperation with South Korea and other countries. Direct benefits include creation of infrastructure and facilities, employee wages paid by South Korea or foreign companies, sale of raw materials, and development of related industries and neighboring areas. Indirect benefits include attraction of foreign capital, improved country risk ratings, and ease of economic sanctions by the U.S. and allies.

THE FUTURE OF NORTH KOREA

As with East and West Germany when the Berlin Wall fell in 1989, it is difficult to predict when and how the two Koreas will be united. However, most experts think that there are three broad alternative outcomes: war, a North Korean collapse, or the continuation of a two-state peninsula (Noland 1998). However, one can break down the future of North Korea into five scenarios of change: unification through the military defeat of North Korea, unification through the collapse of North Korea, continuation of the status quo, reform without the regime change, and reform with the regime change.

North and South Koreas may be united by a war. Will North Korea attack the South? This has been one of the key questions for the U.S. and South Korea in attempting to develop trilateral relations with the country over five decades. The usual argument for this possibility is that North Korean leaders will have no options but war against the South when their regime collapses. A conventional attack by North Korea, however, is highly unlikely as long as the U.S. security umbrella over South Korea remains intact and North Korea receives economic assistance from South Korea, Japan, and other countries. Should North Korea launch a conventional attack, the combined forces of the U.S. and South Korea would be free to retaliate, which is likely to end the existence of North Korea.

If North Korea faces political and economic problems beyond its control, no one can deny the possibility that North Korea will invade South Korea out of desperation. In fact, North Korea has repeatedly stated that if they have to go under, they will drag South Korea along. Seoul's location just 25 miles south of the demilitarized zone makes it virtually impossible to protect from initial artillery attacks. Even with modern antibattery guided weapons, the greater Seoul metropolitan area could not escape damage that would wreak havoc where about a third of the South Korean population makes a living.

The North Korean collapse is the most undesirable outcome for North Korean leadership, who will thus try to avoid it at all costs. Moreover, South Korea might not want to absorb North Korea for a variety of reasons, such as the enormous cost of unification and the possible social chaos from a massive migration of Northerners into the already crowded South. In fact, some analysts believe that South Korea would try to prevent the collapse of North Korea, if its regime appears to be teetering. South Korea's sunshine policy toward North Korea and help from the West may preserve the longevity of the North Korean regime for quite some time. Nevertheless, some analysts believe that North Korea will eventually collapse mainly due to three sets of economic problems. The first concerns the stresses faced by war economies—economic systems of total war mobilization. The second involves severe exogenous economic shocks to centrally planned economies. Historically, such shocks have generated not only systemwide crises such as the collapse of the Soviet Union but also international sanctions or wartime embargoes. The third set of problems pertains to the stresses attendant to dealing with food shortages under communist economies.

Continuation of the status quo must also be counted among

North Korea's future scenarios. Certainly, this is the option that North Korean leaders want most. When Kim Il Sung died in 1994, some experts suggested a time frame of two or three years within which North Korea must either fatefully choose (or attack South Korea) or fall apart. However, now many people believe that North Korea's remarkable survival skills will enable it to continue to survive without overhauling its political-economic structure. North Korea has maneuvering room in foreign policy because the five governments that must contend most directly with Pyongyang— Seoul, Washington, Beijing, Tokyo, and Moscow—do not want an abrupt shift in the status quo.

Reform without the regime change has been going on for some time. First, North Korean leaders seem to have realized that they can no longer ignore domestic and external pressures for change. Second, they may think that they can control the pace of economic liberalization and lessen the danger of an East-German style disintegration. South Korea and the U.S. had felt that the best way to minimize the risk on the Korean peninsula was to offer all possible inducements to North Korea to choose peace and reform. Some fruits of this policy include a 2000 summit between North and South Korean leaders, the 1997 four-party talks, and the 1994 Agreed Framework to end North Korean nuclear weapons program. However, the Bush administration's hardline policy toward North Korea has practically halted many North Korean reforms.

Reform with the regime's change is unlikely any time soon though it may be possible at some point in the future. North Korea must have learned a critical lesson from the East Europe's experience in the early 1990s. That lesson is once you open the floodgate, no one can stop the flow. Thus, North Korean leaders will try to keep the country closed for as long as possible. However, forces for change, such as North Korean economic problems and the growing globalization, are almost impossible to ignore. The North Korean military or a group it supports is most likely to seize power if there is any new regime in the North.

The future of Korea boils down to a struggle for power between the two camps: South Korea, Japan, and the U.S. on one hand versus North Korea, China, and Russia on the other. The former bloc has so far been leading in the game of influence. On the other hand, North Korea's supporters have been in no position to contest the military and economic superiority of the West since the end of the Cold War. However, China and Russia will stand by the North Korean regime to prevent any radical changes on the peninsula. Clearly, South Korea, Japan, and the U.S. prefer that North Korea liberalize its economy. North Korea knows that such reforms may contain the seeds of its defeat or demise. The painful fact is that North Korean patrons—China and Russia—may not have the ability either to withstand the pressures from the Western camp or to match the assistance it offers. Nevertheless, analysts believe that North Korea is likely to muddle through with support from China, Japan, and South Korea, which would like to avoid its collapse (Norland, 1997).

CONCLUSION

North Korea is a nation of some 22 million people living in a mostly mountainous area the size and approximate latitude of New York state. Recent modest changes in this modern-day hermit kingdom signal a commitment to the kinds of reform that most other communist and former communist states have adopted.

Early in the 1990s, North Korea was abandoned by its former sponsors and allies, Russia and China. Following the death of the founding leader in 1994, North Korea was hard pressed politically and economically, unable to halt the slide in its sinking economy or to feed its people. The dead leader's eldest son, Kim Jong Il, has assumed leadership of North Korea since then, but he has been unable or unwilling to implement extensive reforms.

Although the barriers between East and West have come down almost everywhere else since 1990, Korea remains the Cold War's last holdout. The Korean demilitarized zone continues to be the focal point of the most powerful concentrations of opposing military forces of the post–Cold War world, despite both secret and open attempts at reconciliation. Close to 2 million troops, including 37,000 from the U.S., which would be instantly involved in new hostilities, are on duty in North or South Korea. Today American overseas commitments and military forces are at greater risk at the Korean demilitarized zone than anywhere else.

North Korean leaders know that atomic bombs and missiles get the West's attention. In fact, engagement may be the only sensible diplomatic solution for dealing with countries that have nuclear weapons and missiles. The North Korean drive to normalize relations with the U.S. represents the single greatest opportunity to stabilize the situation on the Korean peninsula. Since 1988, when this policy was formulated, North Korea prepared to compromise and make concessions when necessary. The proper U.S. response under such circumstances was to forge a comprehensive policy that included South Korea, economic assistance on a large scale, and extensive people-to-people exchanges in a wide variety of fields.

Relations between the U.S. and North Korea reached a high point in the final months of the Clinton administration. That culminated in the visit to Pyongyang by then Secretary of State Madeleine Albright, the highest level U.S. official to travel to the North. Her visit came just a few months after the landmark Pyongyang summit between North and South Korean leaders, Kim Dae Jung and Kim Jong Il, raising hopes of a final peace deal on the Korean peninsula. George W. Bush took the oath of office as the U.S. president in January 2001 and made known his intention to revert to a tougher line on relations. In the past, the State Department labeled North Korea, Iraq, and Iran as a "rogue states" whose military policy and support of other groups threatens Washington's security. In his State of the Union address on January 29, 2002, Bush labeled these three countries as the "axis of evil," thus extending his war on terrorism. This hardline stand under the Bush leadership has effectively worsened U.S.–North Korean relations since then. Many observers argue that North Korea, one of the world's poorest, most isolated countries, is a difficult place to employ the containment, because the world has little left to withdraw or withhold from the country.

KEY TERMS AND CONCEPTS

Taliban
Korean War
World War II
United Nations (UN)
UN Commission on North
  Korea (UNCK)
38th parallel
Berlin Wall
Military Armistice Commission
  (MAC)
Neutral Supervisory Commis-
  sion (NSC)
30-year Treaty of Friendship,
  Alliance, and Mutual Assis-
  tance

Non-Proliferation Treaty
  (NPT)
International Atomic Energy
  Agency (IAEA)
Central Intelligence Agency
  (CIA)
Agreed Framework
Korean Energy Development
  Organization (KEDO)
Ballistic missile
Warhead
Four-party talks
Bipolar confrontation
Sunshine policy
Berlin Declaration

QUESTIONS AND APPLICATION

1. What historical events explain the political tensions that exist between North and South Korea?

2. What is the role of the Military Armistice Commission in Korea?

3. Explain the nature and role of the Korean Energy Development Organization (KEDO).

4. What is the sunshine policy? Why was this policy initially perceived as a threat by North Korea?

5. How was the North Korean economy affected by the collapse of the communist bloc?

6. What are the five possible outcomes for the future of North Korea?

7. Jimmy Carter and Kim Dae Jung have a number of things in common. List and discuss them in some detail.

REFERENCES

Bracken, Paul. *Fire in the East.* New York: Perennial, 1999.

Breen, Michael. *The Koreans.* New York: St. Martin's Press, 1998.

Buss, Claude A. *The United States and the Republic of Korea: Background for Policy.* Hoover International Studies, Hoover Institution Press, Stanford, California: Stanford University, 2002.

Carter, Jimmy. "North Korea." *Washington Post,* Jan. 14, 2003, op-ed page.

Cha, Victor D. "The Rationale for Enhanced Engagement of North Korea." *Asian Survey,* November/December 1999, pp. 845–866.

Christenson, Richard A. "North Korea's Economic Development: An Agenda for Cooperation." In The Korea Economic Institute of America, *The Political Economy of Korean Reconciliation and Reform.* Washington, D.C.: KEI, 2000, pp. 51–58.

Cummings, Bruce. *Korea's Place in the Sun.* New York: W.W. Norton, 1997.

Eberstadt, Nicholas. "Disparities in Socioeconomic Development in Divided Korea." *Asian Survey,* November/December 2000, pp. 867–893.

Harrison, Selig S. "Time to Leave Korea?" *Foreign Affairs,* March/April 2001, pp. 62–78.

Harvey, Joe. "N Korea Hits Back at Bush's Evil Tag." CNN.com./WORLD, February 1, 2002.

Kim Dae Jung. "Reconcile, Cooperate, and Live in Peaceful Coexistence." *Presidents and Prime Ministers,* November/December 2000, pp. 22–24.

Korea Economic Institute of America, ed. *Korea's Economy 2001.* Vol 17. Washington, D.C.: KEI, 2001.

_____. *The Political Economy of Korean Reconciliation and Reform.* Washington, D.C.: KEI, 2001.

Korean Overseas Information Service. *Focus on Korea: This Is Korea.* Seoul: Seoul International Publishing House, 1986.

Lee, Doowon. "The Economic Outlook for Reconciliation and Reunification." In Kongdon Oh and Ralph Hassig, *Korea Briefing.* New York: M.E. Sharpe, 2002, pp. 43–76.

Mazarr, Michael J. "Predator States and War: The North Korea Case." In Dong Whan Park, ed., *The United States and Two Koreas: A New Triangle.* Boulder: Lynne Rienner Publishers, 1998, pp. 75–96.

1. NORTH KOREA

Noland, Marcus. "Why North Korea Will Muddle Through." *Foreign Affairs,* July/August 1997, 105–117.

_____, ed. *Economic Integration of the Korean Peninsula.* Washington, D.C.: Institute for International Economics, January 1998.

Oberdorfer, Don. *The Two Koreas.* New York: Basic Books, 1997.

Oh, Kongdan, and Ralph C. Hassig. "North Korea Between Collapse and Reform." *Asian Survey,* March/April 1999, pp. 287–309.

_____, and _____. *North Korea Through the Looking Glass.* Washington, D.C.: Brookings Institution Press, 2000.

Olson, Edward A. "U.S. Security Policy and the Two Koreas." *World Affairs,* Spring 2000, pp. 150–157.

Park, Dong Whan, ed. *The U.S. and the Two Koreas.* Boulder: Lynne Rienner Publishers, 1988.

Park, Philip. "The Future of the Democratic People's Republic of Korea." *Journal of Contemporary Asia,* Vol. 31, No. 1, 2000, pp. 104–120.

Ratnesar, Romesh. "How Dangerous Is North Korea? *Time,* January 13, 2003, pp. 21–29.

Rubin, Michael. "Don't Engage Rogue Regimes." *The Wall Street Journal,* December 12, 2001, p. A18.

Slavin, Barbara. "Critics Question Tough Talk on Iran, North Korea." *USA Today,* January 31, 2002, p. 8A.

_____, and Laurence McQuillan. "Axis of Evil Scoffs at Speech." *USA Today,* January 31, 2002, p. 1A.

Swomley, John M. "North Korea's Military Threat Has Been Exaggerated." In William Dudley, ed., *North and South Korea.* New York: Greenhaven Press, 2002, pp. 26–33.

Wolffe, Richard. "Who Is the Bigger Threat?" *Newsweek,* January 13, 2003, pp. 22–30.

PART II

North Korea at a Crossroads

Today North Korea stands at the crossroads between continuing survival and collapse. This part looks back at the Korean War because a general knowledge of the historical context is crucial to understanding the current North Korean situation. In addition, it analyzes how North Korea applies Confucianism and self-reliance for its continuing survival. Further, it critically evaluates the roads to Korean unification.

2 The Korean War (1950–1953): Causes and Consequences

SUMMARY

An Armistice Agreement signed on July 27, 1953, by the United States, South Korea, China, and North Korea ended the Korean War (1950–1953), creating a four-mile wide demilitarized zone (DMZ) from one coast of Korea to the other roughly along the 38th parallel. Since that time the world has witnessed the dramatic dissolution of the Soviet Union, the peaceful reunification of Germany and the end of the Cold War. However, the Korean peninsula remains a serious source of threat and conflict in Asia. In fact, the basic structure of Korea's national division has not changed much for half a century. Many experts regard the DMZ as the world's most dangerous flashpoint. During a visit to the DMZ in 1994, U.S. President Bill Clinton was moved to call it "the scariest place on earth." The frangibility of Northeast Asian security is underscored by 1.1 million North Korean troops and by the development of weapons of mass destruction. An understanding of the causes and consequences of the Korean War is essential to comprehend the implications of the current conflict that has embroiled the U.S. and the Korean peninsula.

JAPANESE COLONIAL AMBITIONS

Korea was known as both the "Land of Morning Calm" and the "Hermit Kingdom" for much of its history because of its physical and cultural isolation. Korea is a peninsula attached to northeast Asia. It runs in a southerly direction. Only at its extreme north does the Korean peninsula come into contact with foreign countries. Although Korea was little known to much of the West until the Korean War, Koreans have a well-developed cultural and national identity spanning more than 5,000 years. Even with its physical isolation, for much of its history Korea has been dominated to varying degrees by China, Japan and the Soviet Union. The Korean peninsula's location serves as a natural link among these three great powers. Consequently, the concept of government in Korean history has been based on Confucian tradition for more than 500 years. During the Choson Kingdom period (1392–1910—known by the dynastic name of Yi), the government was led by Confucian scholars, who believed that worldly authority was conferred by a "Mandate of Heaven." Good government guaranteed proper relationships in an authoritarian hierarchical social order with the king at the top of the pyramid. It was a government of the elite and the wealthy *yangban* class of nobility.

This traditional monarchic government was abolished in 1910 when Japan annexed Korea as a colony. The Japanese emperor stated in his Imperial Prescript of 1910 that the Koreans would be treated as Japanese subjects. However, the Japanese instead established a colonial government called the Government-General of Korea, and ruled Korea as a colony. All Governors-General were Japanese army leaders who exercised judicial, legislative and administrative power; they were also empowered to mobilize Japanese troops in Korea.

During their occupation of Korea, the Japanese pursued a ruthless policy of cultural suppression in which Japanese culture was forced upon the Korean people. Japanese was the only language taught in schools, and Korean history was not included in the curriculum. Freedom of speech, press and assembly were taken away from Koreans. Many private schools and all Korean language newspapers and presses were closed down. Koreans were coerced into adopting Japanese names. Korean men were conscripted not only into the Japanese armed forces, but also to work at Japanese mines and factories during World War II.

During the period of colonization, Japan did not attempt to industrialize or modernize the Korean economy. Nor was there professional training for Korean citizens. While the infrastructure in Korea was marginally improved during the Japanese occupation, the economy remained largely agrarian and subservient to the needs of Japan. Korea's resources were exploited by the Japanese without concern for proper resource management over the long term. Additionally, the high taxes imposed by the Japanese government left little capital for investment in the economy. Japanese citizens would eventually expropriate almost 80 percent of Korea's farmlands.

The Koreans, who suffered particularly oppressive and humiliating treatment at the hands of the Japanese during the decade of 1910–1919, desperately sought opportunities to regain their freedom and restore national independence. Even in the darkest period of their history, the Koreans refused to abandon hope as they struggled against extreme odds. Thus, attempts to create an independent Korea continued during the Japanese occupation. Early in 1919, after World War I ended, the opportunity for the Korean people to reassert their right to freedom seemed to have arrived. A major impetus to this Korean independence movement was American President Woodrow Wilson's call for the right of "self-determination" for subjugated people at the Paris Peace Conference. A provisional Korean government was organized in Shanghai, China, to fight for independence. Efforts to obtain Korea's independence reached their peak at the March First Independence Movement of 1919. The movement began when a group of Korean patriots drafted and proclaimed Korea's independence at a place in Seoul that many foreigners now call Pagoda Park. Some two million Koreans participated in a peaceful demonstration against the Japanese, and many more engaged in civil disobedience in support of independence.

Japan's response to the independence movement was immediate and brutal. Japanese police killed 25,000 Koreans, wounded tens of thousands, burned down thousands of Korean homes and Christian church buildings, and imprisoned some 50,000 Korean nationals. A 17-year-old female student named Yu Kwan-sun was brutally tortured by Japanese police and died in prison, but she galvanized a fervent patriotism among young Korean students through her suffering (Nahm, 1983, p. 96). Nevertheless, Korea was unable to win its independence for many years. Japan's imperialism continued in Korea until Japan was defeated by the Allies in World War II.

THE DIVISION OF KOREA

In much of the world, the best-known fact about the Koreans is that they are a divided people. For 1,300 years, they had lived in a single state roughly along a border with China. In 1945, however, their peninsula was divided into two separate zones. The dividing line was drawn by two American officials at the 38th parallel as a convenient halfway point for Soviet and American armies to meet and accept the Japanese surrender (Breen, 1998, p. 116).

The Korean people had suffered under Japanese occupation. With the close of World War II, Koreans were looking forward to their long-cherished dream of independence. At the Cairo Conference of 1943, the Allied Forces of the United States, Great Britain, and China had agreed that Korea would become an independent nation "in due course." To Koreans this meant the welcome exit of the Japanese. However, in a treaty at Yalta in early 1945, the Soviet Union agreed to enter the war against Japan. In return for its assistance in the war, the Soviet Union would be permitted to disarm Japanese troops in the northern half of the Korean peninsula. The real cause for the partition of Korea at the Yalta Agreement was never clarified. Americans at this time did not seem to understand the totality of the communist doctrine and governmental system. The Soviet Union swooped rapidly into North Korea at the close of the war.

When the Japanese surrender finally came, the U.S. and the Soviet Union agreed that U.S. forces would occupy South Korea, and Soviet troops would occupy North Korea. This occupation was intended to be a temporary arrangement until elections, supervised by the United Nations (UN), would be held to form a single, unified government for Korea. The U.S.-Soviet Joint Commission held a series of meetings in 1946 and 1947, but failed to reach an agreement about the timetable for elections or withdrawal from North and South Korea. Then, in September 1947, the UN General Assembly adopted a resolution to hold general elections in Korea to insure immediate independence and unification. However, the Soviet Union and its communist followers in the North refused to comply with the UN resolution and barred the UN Commission on Korea (UNCK) from entering North Korea.

In order to accomplish its mission in Korea, UNCK carried out national elections on the peninsula south of the 38th parallel on May 10, 1948. On August 15, 1948, the government of the Republic of Korea (South Korea) was officially proclaimed and Syngman Rhee took the oath of office as the first president of the Republic of Korea. Without UN involvement, North Korean communists held their own "elections" in September 1948. Under the sponsorship of the Soviet Union, Kim Il Sung established the so-called Democratic People's Republic of Korea (North Korea). Thus, the 38th parallel became the metaphorical Berlin Wall in Korea.

CAUSES OF THE KOREAN WAR

During the period from 1946 to 1948, a communist named Kim Il Sung joined with Soviet troops and became a strong man in the North. After crushing all nationalist organizations, Kim became the head of a temporary government in northern Korea (later North Korea) under Soviet supervision. Under the continued tutelage of the Soviet Union, Kim brought about the communization of North Korea. At the same time, democratic principles were introduced during the American rule in South Korea. But soldiers were poor promoters of democracy. Democracy exercised by the Americans allowed the emergence of political and social organizations, including those of the communists. The Korean Communist Party, which became the South Korean Workers' Party, instigated labor strikes, printed counterfeit money, and engaged in other illegal activities. These activities and other social difficulties made the Syngman Rhee government both unpopular and unstable.

After the respective governments in the North and the South were formed, both the U.S. and the Soviet Union reduced their physical presence in their occupied sectors. However, the Soviet Union devoted considerable resources to building the North's military capacity, while the U.S. devoted almost no resources to strengthen the South's military capacity. Despite a request from the South to the U.S. to keep its troops in Korea, the U.S. withdrew its forces from Korea by late summer of 1949. This withdrawal left poorly trained and inadequately equipped Korean armed forces of 96,000 men to defend their national independence under some 500 American military advisors.

The Soviet Union, on the other hand, gave a large amount of up-to-date military equipment to North Korea, including 200 jet fighters and 500 heavy tanks, before it withdrew its troops from the North. South Korea had no such weapons. In addition, some 2,500 Russian military advisors remained in the North to train 175,000 communist troops there. By June 1950, the number of troops in the North grew to 200,000 (Nahm, 1983, p.104). With growing military strength and supported by the Soviet Union, North Korea increased its threats to the Republic in the South.

On January 12, 1950, Dean Acheson, the U.S. Secretary of State, disclosed in a speech at the National Press Club in Washington D.C., that South Korea was outside the U.S. defense perimeter. His speech was viewed as a green light by the North Korean communists to cross the 38th parallel. The combination of popular dissatisfaction with the Syngman Rhee government and the unfortunate statement by Dean Acheson caused the leaders of North Korea to believe a war to unite the country under its auspices could be won.

The Korean War

On the morning of June 25, 1950, North Korea attacked South Korea, captured the South Korean capital of Seoul within four days, and subsequently overran two-thirds of South Korea within a month. Five days after the North Korean invasion, American President Henry S Truman sent American air and naval forces to assist South Korea. A few days later, he authorized the bombing of specific targets in North Korea, approved the use of ground forces, and started a naval blockade of the entire Korean coast.

Both South Korean and U.S. forces took a last stand in the Pusan region in the southeastern corner of the peninsula. Realizing the grave danger to South Korea's existence, Truman requested the assistance of the UN. The Security Council of the UN condemned North Korea as an aggressor and asked UN member nations to provide military and other assistance for South Korea. Consequently, troops from the U.S. and 15 other nations organized UN forces and joined the South Korean forces. U.S. Army General Douglas MacArthur was placed in command of the UN forces. The UN forces launched a counterattack against North Korean forces as additional U.S. forces and troops from Great Britain, France, Canada, Australia and other countries arrived in Korea.

On September 15, 1950, UN forces made a successful amphibious assault far behind North Korean lines at Inchon near Seoul and conquered North Korean forces in the South. This surprise amphibious landing at Inchon struck the North Korean army at its flank and severed supply lines. The UN forces recaptured Seoul on September 28. Under the authorization given by the UN and the U.S. government, U.S. and South Korean troops crossed the 38th parallel in pursuit of fleeing North Korean troops. The UN forces captured the North Korean capital of Pyongyang on October 19, 1950, and quickly pressed north along the peninsula as far as the Yalu River, which marks Korea's border with China.

To prevent the defeat of North Korea, however, 150,000 Chinese troops poured into Korea in the middle of October from Manchuria and pushed the UN forces back to the 38th parallel. The UN forces withdrew from North Korea during the winter of 1950 and abandoned Seoul to the aggressors on January 4, 1951. Inconclusive but fierce fighting continued for a few months, but the tide of the war gradually turned against North Korea.

North Korea proposed a truce through the Soviet Union, and talks began between the representatives of the two sides in the summer of 1951. However, truce negotiations progressed slowly for nearly two years. With the death of the Soviet dictator Joseph Stalin in early 1953, the North Koreans were anxious to end the war. As a result, an Armistice Agreement was signed on July 27, 1953, creating a four-mile wide demilitarized zone across the peninsula. With this, the truce village of Panmunjom was put on the Korean map. Before the Korean War, Panmunjom was a small farming village, but it has become the meeting place of the Korean Armistice Commission and infrequent contacts between North and South Korean representatives. To this date, a Military Armistice Commission (MAC) and a Neutral Nations Supervisory Commission (NSC) continue to supervise the truce. The MAC is composed of five officers from North and South Korea to supervise the armistice and settle any violations through negotiations. The NSC consists of officers from Sweden, Switzerland, Poland, and Czechoslovakia, who carry out specific functions of supervision, observation, inspection, and investigation.

CONSEQUENCES OF THE KOREAN WAR

North Korea's ambition to conquer South Korea by force fortunately failed, but the war caused enormous property damage and more than 1.6 million combat casualties. Nearly 147,000 South Korean forces and 35,000 UN soldiers died during the bitter three-year war. North Korean and Chinese forces suffered approximately 1.42 million casualties over the same period (Korean Overseas Information Service, 1986, p. 35). These figures, however, cannot convey the horrors that the war inflicted on the Korean people. Even 50 years later, the South remains concerned over possible military actions by the North.

The Korean War left the territory controlled by South Korea in ruins. The city of Seoul was particularly devastated, since it had changed hands four times during the course of the three-year war. Little of the city remained standing. More than 60 percent of South Korea's industrial facilities were destroyed. Property damage was estimated at $3 billion, equal to the nation's combined income for 1952 and 1953. The war also caused enormous social dislocation, as 380,000 Korean civilians were killed in war-related actions (Griffin, 1988). Families were separated and scattered throughout Korea. Countless orphans, widows, and severely injured veterans were left to pick up the pieces of a shattered society. No one knows for sure how much North Korea suffered from the war economically, but most experts believe that its economic damage was more severe than that of South Korea.

After the end of the Korean War, the U.S. adopted a general policy of military containment, diplomatic isolation, and economic sanctions against North Korea. In order to prevent another war, Washington signed a mutual security treaty with Seoul in 1953. Furthermore, to implement its anticommunist containment policy in Asia, the U.S. signed a series of bilateral and multilateral security treaties with South Korea, Japan, the Philippines, Thailand and New Zealand. However, the U.S.-led coalition with Japan and Korea faced a counter-alliance between North Korea, the Soviet Union and China.

In the 30-year Treaty of Friendship, Alliance and Mutual Assistance signed in February 1950, Russia and China agreed to use "necessary means" to prevent the revival of Japanese imperialism. This Sino-Soviet treaty served as a model for North Korea's mutual defense treaties with the Soviet Union and China that were signed in 1961. These treaties by two rival camps fully integrated the Korean peninsula into the Cold War bipolar framework (Eberstadt and Ellings, 2001, pp. 56–61).

For nearly half a century following the Korean War, the nature of the economic linkages between the U.S. and North Korea could be easily described in a single word: nonexistent. Three days after the outbreak of the Korean War, the U.S. Congress approved legislation to ban all exports to North Korea. Over the next four decades, the scope and specificity of U.S. legal sanctions against commercial and financial transactions steadily expanded. By the early 1990s, possibilities for any economic contact between the two countries were proscribed by at least 10 separate laws (Davis, 1994).

In the first years following the Korean War, the centrally-directed economy of North Korea had been larger in per capita income and had grown more rapidly than the more loosely-controlled economy of South Korea. However, in the absence of rational and strategic economic planning, these advantages soon reached their limits. By the mid–1970s, South Korea's two successful five-year economic plans put it ahead of North Korea. One of the most densely populated countries in the world, South Korea has few natural resources. The phenomenal economic growth of South Korea for the last two decades, however, has led commentators to call it a little Japan, another Japan, or the next Japan. In fact, South Korea has been officially recognized as an industrialized country since 1996 when the country joined the Organization for Economic Cooperation and Development (OECDE). Moreover, South Korea has enjoyed a stable, democratic government since the late 1980s. As a result, the country plays an increasingly important role in the world economy.

North Korea is a society governed by an absolute ruling ideology called *juche*, a concept of autonomy and self-sufficiency that leads to the belief that Korea should be free from any foreign intervention. North Korea's economy prominently applies this ideology, which means the economy is socialized and centrally planned. Confucianism is another guiding principle for North Korea. Confucianism is not technically a religion, but rather an ethical and moral system explicitly regulating the proper conduct of social relationships. Under Confucian teachings, an inferior is expected to be obedient to his superior, and the superior to be benevolent to his inferior. This model caused the North Korean society to produce ever-loyal disciples of the leader, and glorified the solidarity of the people as a modern Confucian family around the Communist Party and its leader.

Early in the 1990s, North Korea was abandoned by its former sponsors and allies, the Soviet Union and China. Kim Il Sung, who was installed in power by Joseph Stalin in 1948, had controlled North Korea until his death. Prior to and following Kim's death in 1994, North Korea was hard pressed politically and economically, unable to halt the deterioration of its economy or adequately feed its people. Kim Il Sung's eldest son, Kim Jong Il, has since assumed leadership of North Korea, creating the communist bloc's first dynastic succession. However, North Korea has been slipping badly by virtually every indicator since the Soviet Union collapsed in 1990.

Many people had been concerned about the danger of an attack by North Korea until the mid–1980s. However, a series of events since the late 1980s transformed the relations among the two Koreas and four Pacific powers from confrontation to greater cooperation. The four Pacific powers—China, Japan, Russia and the U.S.—significantly expanded the scope of their cooperation in military, diplomatic, and economic fields. South Korea increased the level of cooperation with these four powers during the same period. Even North Korea gradually improved its relations with South Korea, Japan and the U.S. until President George W. Bush labeled North Korea as part of the "axis of evil" in his State of the Union address on January 29, 2002. That remark by President Bush, along with subsequent events, has played a central role in stalling many reforms in North Korea and its dialogue with key U.S. allies.

Key Terms and Concepts

Demilitarized zone	Paris Peace Conference
Yangban	Provisional government
Colony	Pagoda Park
Imperial Prescript of 1910	The Cairo Conference of 1943
Government-General of Korea	Yalta Conference

Questions and Application

1. Which countries have historically influenced or dominated Korea and what is the most obvious common reason for these dominations?

2. What form of government replaced the 500-year-old Choson monarchic rule in Korea in the early 20th century?

3. Why did the Japanese colonization of Korea encounter resistance? Was the Government-General of Korea able to remedy the Japanese shortcomings in Korea?

4. How did President Woodrow Wilson's speech at the 1919 Paris Peace Conference affect the Japanese colonial rule in Korea? Explain the events that followed.

5. Explain how the Yalta Conference influenced the separation of the Koreas. Was the outcome planned or was it the result of poor strategic planning and foresight?

6. Describe the political climate in North and South Korea shortly before the Korean War. What respective roles did the Soviet Union and the United States play in the events that led to the Korean War?

7. UN troops successfully defeated North Korean invaders out of South Korea and pushed them as far back as the borders separating the North from China. What prevented the Korean unification at that time?

8. Name one way in which the Korean War strengthened the North Korean political and economic position and one way in which it weakened it.

References

Breen, Michael. *The Koreans.* New York: St. Martin's Press, 1998, p. 116.

Cummings, Bruce. *Korea's Place in the Sun.* New York: W.W. Norton 1997.

Davis, Zachary S. "Korea: Procedural and Jurisdictional Questions Relating to a Possible Normalization of Relations with North Korea." Washington, D.C.: Congressional Research Service, November 24, 1994.

Griffin, Trenholme J. *Korea: The Tiger Economy.* London: Euromoney Publications, 1988.

International Council of Korean Studies. *International Journal of Korean Studies,* Spring/Summer 2001.

Korean Overseas Information Service. *Focus on Korea.* Seoul: Seoul International Publishing House, 1986.

Lee, Chae-Jin. "Conflict and Cooperation: The Pacific Powers and Korea." In Eberstadt, Nicholas, and Richard J. Ellings, eds., *Korea's Future and Great Powers.* Seattle: National Bureau of Asian Research, 2001, pp. 51–87.

Moon, Chung In, Odd Arne Westad, and Gyoo Hyoung Kahng, eds. *Ending the Cold War in Korea.* Seoul: Yonsei University Press, 2001.

Nahm, Andrew C. *A Panorama of 5,000 Years: Korean History.* Elizabeth, N.J.: Holly International Corp., 1983, p. 104.

3 North Korea's Continuing Survival: The Pathway of Confucianism and Self-reliance

SUMMARY

The end of the Cold War in 1990 and the onset of food shortages strengthened the widespread belief that just like East Germany, North Korea was doomed to collapse. This belief's persistence, especially on the part of the United States and its allies, is the main reason why they failed to develop a coherent long-term policy toward North Korea. Instead, they have relied on short-term fixes while waiting for North Korea's collapse. Admittedly, there may be several similarities in recent histories of Korea and Germany, even commonalities in the last 50 years, but North Korea's collapse is unlikely any time soon (Harrison, 2002, pp. 21–24). Similarities between Korea and Germany include the division of homogeneous societies, the Cold War and its alliance system, tensions between a communist dictatorship and a capitalist democratic system, and a sense of national identity deeply uprooted by war. However, when predicting a collapse, many observers ignore the cultural and historical differences that set the two nations apart. The Soviet occupation imposed an alien totalitarian model in East Germany, but North Korea's totalitarianism was guided by unique principles based on Confucianism and the concept of self-reliance. This chapter explains why the two guiding principles might enable North Korea to enjoy longevity contrary to widespread assumptions that the country will collapse in the conceivable future.

CONFUCIANISM

Confucius, the famous sage of China, was born in 550 B.C. when the empire experienced a national crisis caused by corruption, decay, anarchy, and social chaos. Confucius was frightened by what he saw and undertook the work of reformation. Confucianism, being a way of life or a philosophy rather than a rigid religion, fosters an ideal ethical-moral system intended to govern five relationships within the family and the state in harmonious unity (Griffin, 1998, p. 9). These five relationships teach that: (1) between father and son, there should be affection; (2) between ruler and subject, righteousness; (3) between husband and wife, attention to separate functions; (4) between old and young, proper order and respect; and (5) between friends, faithfulness. The most important point in the first four relationships is that there is dominance on one side (ruler, father, husband, and old) and submission on the other side (subject, son, wife, and young).

Korea is a country built on relationships. All social and business interaction is structured on the basis of the relationships of parties involved, and this basis centers on the view that one person is considered superior to another. Several factors determine which person has superior status, and they are so extensive that there is nearly always something, which distinguishes any two individuals. Even in the case of twins, the first-born will have superior status. While the determination of relevant status is complex, any Korean can immediately sense his or her place in the social hierarchy.

Confucius had 3,000 professed disciples, many of whom were seldom long away from him. They stood or sat by his side, watched his conduct, and studied a variety of things under his direction, and treasured every syllable he taught. Future generations inherited his books, volumes of commentary, including dialogues between himself and his disciples. Confucius and his followers visited many parts of the country to advise the dukes and princes on the right way to govern. However, Confucius had never held a government post to test his theories, living most of his life as a wandering scholar-teacher.

The philosophy of Confucius had never embraced supernatural questions and left human affairs strictly alone as long as relative order and good government prevailed on earth. In this respect, Confucianism was a religion without a god and filled a social function of religion at that time. However, as ages passed, followers raised the sage and his disciples to veneration in an effort to spread their doctrines among simple and common people.

Confucianism, introduced sometime in the 4th century, greatly influenced political and social orders in Korea throughout its history. It was accepted so eagerly and strictly that the Chinese themselves regarded Korea as "the country of Eastern decorum" (Yoon, 1986, p. 137). Confucianism influenced education, ceremony, and civil administration. More specifically, it became the guiding precept for the state, presiding over progress in social reform and developing judicial systems. Because the deeply ingrained legacy of Confucianism is still an important feature of Korean life, academics attempt to make Confucian values more relevant to a modern, industrial society. It stresses reverence for learning and culture, social stability, and respect for the past. Its tradition includes the worship of ancestors, the continuation of the bloodline, the proper burial of the matriarchs and patriarchs of the family.

The proper burial of an ancestor is so important that "moving an ancestor's grave is one of the most important decisions one can make in Korean tradition. Because the final resting place of the dead is believed to influence the fate of future descendents, ancestral remains are sometimes moved to a more propitious location several years after interment. This is especially true if a lack of preparation or a lack of financial resources mandated less than suitable arrangements at the time of death" (Linton, 1997). Respect for the dead also comes in the form of continued ancestral rites and memorial ceremonies. Many Koreans hold memorial rites for their deceased parents just before an important event, based on the belief that the parents can help them obtain their desires. South Korea held its 16th presidential election on December 19, 2002. The presidential candidates of the major political parties visited their parents' graves that morning. In effect, they were asking the dead to help them become elected as the next president of South Korea.

Besides a strong traditional force in the past, Confucianism's ethical requirements impinge on the way average Koreans think and act. Children must obey their parents and teachers; wives are at the command of their husbands; and at work, a hierarchy of juniors to seniors is rigorously maintained. Confucian virtues are benevolence for juniors, respect for seniors, and reciprocity between a kindly ruler and his obedient followers. Accordingly, North Korea has constantly depicted Kim Il Sung and Kim Jong Il as benevolent fathers of the nation, comparing the country itself to one large family. Appeals for support use metaphors designed to draw on the feelings of duty toward one's parents, seeking to transfer these feelings to a national father figure (Harrison, 2002, p. 21).

Despite a half century of Marxism, North Korea still consciously appropriates the powerful Confucian traditions of political centralization and obedience to authority that date back more than six centuries. The Confucian philosophy teaches that each person has his place in a hierarchical social order and that the preservation of harmony within this social order is of paramount importance. Under Confucian teachings, inferiors are expected to be obedient to superiors and superiors benevolent to inferiors. In practice, the obedience component is emphasized over the benevolence component in order to maintain the status quo. In addition, the emphasis on preserving harmony results in a lack of mobility between levels in the hierarchy. Kim Il Sung and Kim Jong Il have consciously attempted to wrap themselves in the mantle of Confucian virtues. Thus, North Korea's tightly controlled system has lasted longer than any other 20th century dictatorship because its leadership carried over traditions of centralized authority inherited from the Confucian-influenced Korean dynasties of the past.

THE PRINCIPLE OF SELF-RELIANCE

Under the custodianship of Kim Il Sung and Kim Jong Il, *juche* (the principle of self-reliance) guided North Korea's ideology. *Juche* is credited to Kim Il Sung, who is characterized in the 1998 socialist constitution and elsewhere as "a genius ideological theoretician." The first syllable, *ju*, means "the main or fundamental" principle; the second syllable, *che*, means body, self or the foundation of something. Kim introduced *juche* in a speech to the Korean Workers Party as propaganda meant to agitate workers on December 28, 1955, when he was still trying to eliminate rival politicians.

Kim Jong Il transformed *juche* from a nationalistic ruling ideology to a cult ideology. Kim Jong Il was officially introduced as Kim Il Sung's successor in 1980. Not being a soldier, a political leader, or an economist, Kim Jong Il's role was to interpret and propagandize *juche* ideology and oversee cultural affairs. Because he was accountable to no one except his father, Kim Jong Il made *juche* an article of faith rather than a guide on all matters (Oh and Hassig, 2000, p. 201).

North Korea's economy prominently applies to the ideological principle of *juche* under the following three principles. First, the 1998 revision of North Korea's constitution stipulates that all means of production are owned solely by the state and cooperative organizations. All industrial facilities and commercial enterprises are state owned. Most farms operate as collectives under the strict guidance of the party. Under the second economic principle of central planning, the state formulates unified and detailed plans to guarantee a high rate of production growth and balanced development of the national economy. The third economic principle of *juche* is self-sufficiency, that is to say, socialist production relations are based upon the foundation of independent national economy. In accordance with the *juche* principle, North Korea's foreign trade amounts only to around 10 percent of its gross national product, far below that of most other economies.

Kim's speech also revealed a core concept of national self-reliance and pride. Thus, North Korea adapted Marxist-Leninist principles to Korean condition rather than accept them wholesale. However, the Western press ridiculed his appeal to nationalism because during the Korean War China had saved North Korea as a state and Soviet aid rebuilt its economy. Of course, other measures of its dependence, such as reliance on foreign powers for economic aid and military support, eroded belief that North Korea is a self-sufficient state. Consequently, the original idea of self-reliance underwent revisions in the intervening years to make it compatible with evolving interpretations of *juche*. It is not unusual in North Korea to revise original texts for later publication to make them consistent with more recent ideological thought. For North Koreans, *juche* is inseparable from socialism and is considered the only means by which the masses can gain independence. Still, whatever changes evolved in the *juche* concept over the years, North Korea's commitment to socialism as an organizational principle has never changed.

As *juche* developed, the principle addressed several major issues. First, it served to maintain North Korea's independence in the international community. Second, it also modeled North Koreans into ever-loyal disciples of the leader, but at the same time, it gave them an individual purpose as "masters of society." Third, it glorified the solidarity of the people as a modern Confucian family around the party and its leader. Fourth, it defended North Korea's brand of socialism in the face of declining living standards and the collapse of the international communist bloc. Finally, under increasingly miserable conditions in the wake of Kim Il Sung's death, it gave the people a reason to live, even to die for the regime.

It seems that most people support the idea of *juche* as a principle of national sovereignty, pride, and self-sufficiency. National pride and the desire to preserve independence characterize all nations. National self-sufficiency appeals to everyone, even though national economies must operate interdependently. But North Korea has used *juche* to control the masses. *Juche* as a label has been attached to any idea promoted by the Kims. *Juche* farming, for example, prescribes when and how crops are to be planted; *juche* steel dictates the steelmaking process. In all cases, *juche* strives to make local production units self-sufficient as the nation progresses to self-sufficiency. Unfortunately, *juche* ideology functions as an anchor preventing the North Korean state from moving with the times.

Juche, repeated endlessly in classrooms and in the media, emphasizes national self-reliance, independence, and worship of the supreme leader. Although North Koreans often fail to follow the teachings of *juche* in their everyday lives, the ideology remains a powerful influence on their domestic and international policies. Coupled with carry-over from Confucianism, this quasi-religious nationalist mystique explains why the North Korean leadership commands such a broad popular support of its totalitarian regime.

CONCLUSION

In the 1990s, the North Korean economy ground to a halt as its people faced disease and starvation while communist countries elsewhere toppled like dominos. How, in these hard times, did the North Korean masses accept or tolerate socialism and still believe in the greatness of the leader who brought them to ruin? First, the North Korean regime forced people to engage in endless study and self-criticism so that they would be loyal to the leader and the party indefinitely. Second, they have never experienced political or social freedom. During the Choson dynasty, many of them worked for landlords. Shortly after the turn of the century, the entire economy was geared to supply Japan. After World War II, the communists imposed a centralized form of nonparticipatory government.

Finally, the masses in North Korea differ in two important respects from those in the former Soviet Union and Eastern Europe. To the North Korean people, life in an autocratic society is the commonplace norm. Such a life is backed by centuries of Confucian teaching that ordinary people should subject themselves to superiors, who in principle rule as benevolent fathers. Because political ideas are handed down to the people by their leaders, there is no room for discussion or debate other than interminable explanation and elaboration. In addition, they are cut off from outside information in the name of self-reliance. Because North Koreans have little information about life or thought outside their country, they have no points of references if they question what they are told. Even if they were not committed to some ideological points and actually disbelieved others, they had no energy to pursue their own thoughts and no opportunity to discuss them. So, to avoid complicating life, they abandoned political thought and resigned themselves to repeating the political lessons they were taught. Together with the power of nationalism, these basic differences explain why what happened to East Germany is unlikely to be repeated in North Korea in the conceivable future.

KEY TERMS AND CONCEPTS

Cold War   Juche
Confucius   Cooperative organization
Confucianism   Self-reliance
Kim Il Sung   Leninist principles
Kim Jong Il   Choson dynasty
Marxism   Autocratic society

QUESTIONS AND APPLICATION

1. What is Confucianism? What are the five relationships that are described under this philosophy?

2. What are the common principles that link the relationships described by Confucian teachings?

3. How does Confucianism influence the way average Koreans think and act?

4. How has Confucianism been beneficial for communism in North Korea? How has it been a negative force for social reforms?

5. What is meant by the principle of *juche*?

6. Explain how the ideological principles of *juche* apply to North Korea's economic policies.

7. Do most North Koreans support the idea of *juche*? How does this ideology promote or stunt North Korea's economic growth?

REFERENCES

Cummings, Bruce. *Korea's Place in the Sun*. New York: W. W. Norton, 1997.

Griffin, Trenholme J. *Korea: The Tiger Economy*. London: Euromoney Publications, 1988.

Harrison, Selig S. *Korean Endgame*. Princeton, N.J.: Princeton University Press, 2002.

Linton, Stephen. "Life after Death in North Korea." In David McCann, ed., *Korea Briefing: Toward Reunification*. Armonk, N.Y.: East Gate Books, 1997, p. 92.

Natsios, Andrew S. *The Great North Korean Famine*. Washington, D.C.: The United States Institute of Peace Press, 2001.

Oh, Kongdan, and Ralph C. Hassig. *North Korea Through the Looking Glass*. Washington, D.C.: Brookings Institution Press, 2000.

Yoo, Yushin. *Korea the Beautiful: Treasurers of the Hermit Kingdom*. Los Angeles: Golden Press, 1986.

4 Roads to Korean Unification

Summary

The dissolution of the Soviet Union, the German unification, and China's embrace of capitalism have brought neither the collapse of North Korea nor the end of confrontation on the Korean peninsula. Contrary to the predictions of many experts that North Korea would not long survive the loss of its communist allies, the country has defied the "natural laws of politics" for more than 12 years. As with East and West Germany when the Berlin Wall fell in 1989, it is difficult to predict when and how the two Koreas will be united. One can break down the future of North Korea into five scenarios of change: unification through the military defeat of North Korea, unification through collapse of North Korea, continuation of the status quo, reform without regime change, and reform with regime change. However, most experts think that there are three broad alternative outcomes: war, a North Korean collapse, or the continuation of a two-state peninsula with some reform (Noland, 1998).

61

Unification Through the Military Defeat of North Korea

North and South Koreas may be united by a war. Will the North attack the South? This has been one of the key questions for the U.S. and South Korea in attempting to develop trilateral relations with the country for over five decades. The usual argument for this possibility is that North Korean leaders will have no option but war against the South when their regime collapses. A conventional attack by North Korea, however, is highly unlikely as long as the U.S. security umbrella over South Korea remains intact and North Korea receives economic assistance from South Korea, Japan, and other countries. Should North Korea launch a conventional attack, the combined forces of the U.S. and South Korea would be free to retaliate and likely end the existence of North Korea.

If North Korea faces political and economic problems beyond its control, no one can deny the possibility that it will invade South Korea out of desperation. In fact, North Korean leaders have repeatedly stated that if they have to go under, they will drag South Korea along with them. Seoul's location just 25 miles south of the demilitarized zone makes it virtually impossible to protect from initial artillery attacks. Even with modern antibattery-guided weapons, the greater Seoul metropolitan area could not escape damage that would wreak havoc in the city where about a third of the South Korean population makes their living. Scenarios of North Korean provocation involve (1) domestic dilemmas, (2) relations with South Korea and other countries, and (3) military capabilities (Jeon, 1998).

Domestic Dilemmas. The immediate causes of crisis for North Korea are increasing economic problems and continuing food shortages. The North Korean economy began to contract as the collapse of the socialist bloc in 1990 deprived the country of major markets. In fact, North Korea had recorded negative economic growth for nine consecutive years from 1990 to 1998. While enjoying economic benefits from South Korea and other countries, the North Korean economy finally turned around in 1999 and has recorded growth since then. In addition, humanitarian assistance from South Korea, other countries, and international organizations has increased. North Korea, however, does not have sufficient production capacity to accommodate domestic consumption and to compensate for capital depreciation. Consequently, the recent positive economic growth in North Korea is vulnerable and could evaporate at any time. Furthermore, international humanitarian assistance to North Korea has effectively dried up since North Korean officials admitted on October 4, 2002, that they have a uranium-enriching program to make nuclear weapons. This cumulative economic failure presents North Korean leadership with a desperate situation and feeds the anticipation that the regime may initiate some form of armed provocation.

Relations with South Korea and Other Countries. North Korean leader Kim Jong Il has recently exploited South Korea and other countries, in effect duping his foes into solving his regime's crisis. Toward this end, he has demanded, while making military threats, that costly light-water reactors be constructed, food assistance be increased, business investment be made in North Korea, and private economic cooperation be expanded. Because North Korea has lost its base of support in the international community since 1990, its leadership realizes that it has no choice but to approach South Korea and the U.S. for its regime to survive. As a result, many positive changes have taken place in North-South Korean relations since South Korea adopted its sunshine policy of engagement toward North Korea in 1998. Furthermore, relations between the U.S. and North Korea have significantly improved since the 1994 Agreed Framework, in which Washington offered heavy fuel oil and help building nuclear energy plants in exchange for Pyongyang's promise to shut down its nuclear weapons program. However, engagement has already become a hotly contested issue in South Korea, the U.S., and elsewhere since President George W. Bush adopted a hard-line policy toward North Korea in January 2001.

North Korea broke off official contacts with the U.S. when George W. Bush took the oath of office as the U.S. president in

II. North Korean at a Crossroads

January 2001 and made known his intention to revert to a tougher line on relations. Tensions between the two countries have mounted greatly since then. During the first high-level contact after a nearly two-year hiatus, North Korean officials admitted their secret nuclear weapons program to visiting U.S. officials on October 4, 2002. As a result, the U.S. decided, over objection by South Korea and Japan, to suspend oil deliveries to North Korea as punishment for its secret nuclear program. In return, a defiant North Korea announced on December 12, 2002, that it would restart a nuclear reactor it had closed under a 1994 agreement. The country blamed its decision on a U.S. move to end shipments of fuel oil it has used to generate electricity. Military provocation against South Korea may be North Korea's countermeasure to such deteriorating relations between North Korea and other countries.

Military Capabilities. North Korea maintains armed forces and a supply of weapons larger than those of South Korea. North Korea has one of the largest land armies in the world. Its commando force is the largest in the world with nearly 100,000 personnel, 850 fighting and 500 supporting airplanes, and 290 helicopters (Noland 1998, p. 15). In addition, the North has weapons of mass destruction, such as long-range missiles, biological and chemical weapons, several nuclear weapons, and enough enriched uranium to make a few more nuclear bombs. In spite of this numerical superiority, however, many experts believe that North Korea cannot sustain a war or may not launch a war for a variety of reasons. These reasons include its chronic economic problems, the obsolescence of its weapon systems, its lack of logistical support, and shortages of fuel and food. North Korea's proposed strategy of fighting an intensive, all-out war in the shortest period proves their inability to sustain a war. The possibility of an attack by North Korea may depend on the rationality or irrationality of Kim Jong Il. As long as he is given a chance to survive by easing North Korea's current economic problems and solving its food shortages, he will act rationally and thus will not launch a war. However, an all-out war may be possible if Kim realizes that his regime is on the verge of collapse and that he has no other escape from that impasse.

Unification Through the Collapse of North Korea

Observers of North Korean policy predicted the imminent fall of the country just after the Berlin Wall collapsed in 1989. Even optimistic diplomats predicted only seven years, at the most, until collapse (Clifford, 2002). These predictions were partially true for economic collapse, but not for political demise. Nevertheless, many experts believe that the eventual downfall of North Korea is unavoidable unless timely policy changes occur. The collapse of North Korea is the most undesirable outcome for North Korean leadership, who will thus try to avoid it at all costs. Nevertheless, some analysts believe that North Korea will eventually collapse mainly due to three sets of economic problems. The first concerns the stresses faced by war economies—economic systems of total war mobilization. The second involves severe exogenous economic shocks to centrally planned economies. Historically, such shocks have generated not only systemwide crises, such as the collapse of the Soviet Union, but also international sanctions or wartime embargoes. The third set of problems pertains to the stresses attendant to severe food shortages under communist economies.

Economic Systems of Total War Mobilization. Part of North Korea's economic problems has to do with its heavy spending for its military. North Korea's military budget swallows up its civilian budget. North Korea is perhaps the most highly militarized society in the world today. The North has 1.1 million troops, while the South has 700,000 troops. The North has devoted about 25 percent of its economy to its military. On the other hand, the South has spent an average of 2.5 percent on its military. North Korea's economy, furthermore, radically differs from South Korea's. Consider for a moment population size: the North Korean population is half the size of South Korea's and its per capita income is one-seventeenth as large. Evidently, the North is not just smaller, but it is isolated and has a weaker economic base. Military spending by North Korea for years has been so huge that it caused economic decline and eventually food shortages. The North Korean regime understands this problem, but it sees the pursuit of a huge military machine as the only path to security and survival. In other words, with a population less than half that of the South, the North felt compelled to spend more than ten times of its gross national product on defense. This diverted both labor and resources from the development of consumer-oriented light industries. Hence, the very military capability that is supposed to preserve North Korea's national security has become one of the main threats to the country's long-term security.

Economic Shocks to Centrally Planned Economies. The centrally directed economy of North Korea is an inner-directed one. It is centered on building its heavy industry at home while shying away from commitments abroad. Such an economic system proved effective in the early years. Additionally, early economic success had been artificially inflated by massive economic aid and technical assistance from China and the Soviet Union. However, in the absence of rational and strategic economic planning, these advantages soon reached their limits. Predictably, the North Korean economy began to shrink as the collapse of the socialist bloc in 1990 deprived the nation of major markets and economic assistance. Floods in 1995 and 1996 along with a severe drought in 1997 destroyed its inherently inefficient agricultural base. Some observers of North Korea believe that the country's current economic reform is not bold enough to overcome the standard problems of socialist economies, such as inflexible centralized planning, the inefficient use of capital equipment, low productivity, poor quality control, and the lack of incentives for farmers and workers. If current economic woes continue, North Korea will enter a catastrophic phase that will eventually destroy its regime.

Food Shortages. No one knows for sure how many North Koreans have died from food shortages, but international organizations estimate that the number of starving people in North Korea during the 1990s ranged from 1 million to 3 million (Oh and Hassig, 1999, p. 287). The contraction of the North Korean economy, combined with several natural disasters in the 1990s, contributed significantly to the famine. If North Korea continues to refuse peace and reform, humanitarian assistance and other economic aid may dry up and make a dismal economy even worse. At some point, an additional economic disaster, such as another great famine, will have political effects. The collapse of North Korea could come in one of two main ways: from below (its populace) or from above (its leaders). The question is whether the North Korean people will indefinitely starve for their regime. For now, they may buy the regime's argument that their economic hardships have been caused by poor weather and treacherous foreigners. However, it is possible that they will not buy this argument forever. Certainly, it is not easy for people so tightly controlled and weakened by hunger to rebel. If this is the case, the first move may come from the top. The North Korean military or a group it supports are the most likely to rebel and seize power. North Korea may abandon the *juche* (self-reliance) ideology to reform its regime. Furthermore, frustrated by the continuing economic hardship and power struggles among North Korean elites, violent mass uprising, following massive defections to South Korea, Japan, and China, may occur.

Continuation of a Two-State Peninsula with Some Reform

Continuation of a two-state peninsula must also be counted among North Korea's future scenarios. Certainly, this is the option that North Korean leaders want most. When Kim Il Sung died in 1994, some experts suggested a time frame of just a few years within which North Korea must either fatefully choose (or attack South Korea) or fall apart. However, many people believe now that North Korea's remarkable survival skills will enable it to continue to survive without overhauling its political-economic structure. Obviously, there are a number of factors that will help North Korea muddle through. First, North Korea has maneuvering room in foreign policy because the five governments that must contend most directly with Pyongyang—Seoul, Washington, Beijing, Tokyo, and Moscow—do not want an abrupt shift in the status quo. Second, there are two guiding ideologies that make the North Korean collapse unlikely: Confucianism and the principle of self-reliance. Third, the recent economic crisis convinced North Korea to pursue substantive internal reform and external engagement for its own survival.

Maneuvering Room in Foreign Policy. The continued existence of North Korea is a feasible outcome largely because its neighboring countries wish to maintain it as a viable state at the present time. If its neighboring countries pursue more extensive engagement with North Korea, it will likely create fissures within the North Korean polity and hasten internal change in desirable directions. There is some doubt about either the capacity of the North Korean regime to maintain change or the ability of foreign powers to keep North Korea afloat even if they so desire. However, it is important to understand that two principal actors of the North Korean future, South Korea and China, are determined to help North Korea muddle through. South Korea may actually try to prevent the collapse of North Korea because a North Korean collapse would bring insurmountable problems to South Korea, such as the astronomical cost of unification and possible social chaos from a massive migration of Northerners into the already overpopulated South. The two primary objectives of China in this area are to maintain stability and to promote economic development. The emphasis on stability includes support for the continued division of the Korean peninsula and the continued existence of North Korea as a geographic buffer. China tries to promote its economic development by fostering burgeoning trade and investment ties with South Korea. The policy interests of Japan, Russia, and the United States in a gradual process of change on the Korean peninsula parallel those of South Korea and China, emphasizing stability as a primary goal in managing any transition. Such an approach enables four great powers—China, Japan, Russia, and the U.S.—to play a leading role as a stabilizer, protect their military interests in avoiding war on the Korean peninsula, and preserve their economic stakes in the continued prosperity of the region.

Confucianism and Self-Reliance. There are a great number of similarities in the experiences of Korea and Germany for the past half-century, but North Korea's unique guiding principles make its collapse unlikely any time soon (Harrison, 2002). Similarities between Korea and Germany include the division of homogeneous societies, the Cold War and its alliance system, tensions between a communist dictatorship and a capitalist democratic system, and a sense of national identity deeply uprooted by war. However, in predicting a collapse, many observers who compare Korea to Germany ignore the cultural and historical differences that set the two cases apart. The Soviet occupation imposed an alien totalitarian model in East Germany. The principle of self-reliance and Confucian echoes have facilitated totalitarianism in North Korea. *Juche* (self-reliance), repeated endlessly in classrooms and in the media, emphasizes national self-reliance, independence, and worship of the supreme leader. Although North Koreans often fail to follow the teachings of *juche* in their everyday lives, the ideology remains a powerful influence on their domestic and international policies. This quasi-religious nationalist mystique explains why the North Korean leadership is able to command such a broad popular support of its totalitarian discipline. In addition, the North Korean leadership has consciously appropriated the powerful Confucian traditions of political centralization and obedience to authority that date back more than six centuries. Under Confucian teachings, an inferior is expected to be obedient to its superior and a superior to be benevolent to his inferior. Kim Il Sung and Kim Jong Il have consciously attempted to wrap themselves in the mantle of Confucian virtues. Thus, the tightly controlled system of North Korea has lasted longer than any other 20th-century dictatorship because the North Korean leadership carried over traditions of centralized authority inherited from the Confucian-influenced Korean dynasties of the past.

Economic Reform. Loss of allies in the early 1990s and several natural disasters caused the North Korean economy to shrink in the 1990s. It is no wonder why several million North Koreans have died due to starvation and famine-related diseases. While North Korea had gradually reformed its troubled economic system since the early 1990s, these measures were different from market-oriented reform. North Korea introduced them to reinforce the existing centrally planned economic system. Of course, North Korea or any other centrally planned economy cannot achieve sustainable economic growth without market-oriented reform. As a result, North Korea had been widely perceived to be in the poverty trap, implying that it cannot escape without external help. However, in July 2002, North Korea began to introduce the most significant liberalization measures since the start of communist rule in 1948 (French, 2002). Why has North Korea adopted this market-oriented reform all of a sudden? Obviously, North Korea hopes that the transformation of its Marxist economy would allow it to cope with chronic shortages, disease, and starvation. The North Korean leadership clearly understands that its economic reform would not be easy or even dangerous but it offers potentially enormous payoffs. Under favorable conditions, the market-oriented economic reform could probably increase its output by more than half its pre-decline level (Noland, 1997).

Continuation of a two-state peninsula with some reform might or might not involve regime change. Reform without the regime change has been going on for some time. First, North Korean leaders seem to have realized that they can no longer ignore domestic and external pressures for change. Second, they may think that they can control the pace of economic liberalization and lessen the danger of East German–style disintegration. South Korea and its allies have felt that the best way to minimize the risk on the Korean peninsula was to offer all possible inducements to North Korea to choose peace and reform. Some fruits of this policy include a 2000 summit between North and South Korean leaders, the 1997 four-party talks, the 1994 Agreed Framework to end North Korean nuclear weapons program, and the flurry of Pyongyang's recent diplomatic moves to resume dialogue with the U.S. However, the Bush administration's consistent hard-line policy toward North Korea has slowed North Korean reform significantly.

Reform with the regime change is unlikely any time soon though it may be possible at some point in the future. The regime must have learned a critical lesson from East Europe's experience in the early 1990s. That lesson is that once you open the floodgate, no one can stop the flow. Thus, North Korean leaders will try to keep the country closed for as long as possible. However, forces for change, such as North Korean economic problems and the growing globalization, are almost impossible to ignore. The North Korean military or a group it supports is the most likely groups to seize power if there is any new regime in the North.

CONCLUSION

How, when, and whether Korea can be united has confronted both North and South Korea since the division of 1945. This issue shapes their attitudes toward the U.S. North and South Korea alike believe that Washington bears the principal responsibility for the division of the Korean peninsula. Both believe that the U.S. should now accept the principal responsibility for putting the pieces back together.

However, the future of Korea boils down to a struggle for power between two camps: South Korea, Japan, and the U.S. on the one hand versus North Korea, China, and Russia on the other. The former bloc has so far been leading in the game of influence. On the other hand, North Korea's supporters have been in no position to contest the military and economic superiority of the West since the end of the Cold War. However, China and Russia will stand by the North Korean regime to prevent any radical changes on the peninsula. Clearly, South Korea, Japan, and the U.S. prefer that North Korea liberalize its economy. North Korea knows that such reforms may contain the seeds of its defeat or demise. The painful fact is that North Korean patrons—China and Russia—may not have the ability to withstand the pressures from the Western camp or to match the assistance it offers. Nevertheless, analysts believe that North Korea is likely to muddle through with support from China, Japan, and South Korea, all of which would like to avoid its collapse (Norland, 1997).

Moreover, South Korea might not want to absorb North Korea for a variety of reasons, such as the enormous cost of unification and the possible social chaos from a massive migration of Northerners into the already crowded South. In fact, some analysts believe that South Korea would try to prevent the collapse of North Korea if its regime appears to be teetering. South Korea's sunshine policy toward North Korea and Western help may preserve the longevity of the North Korean regime for quite some time.

KEY TERMS AND CONCEPTS

Uranium-enriching program
Light-water reactors (LWR)
Nuclear weapons
Biological weapons
Chemical weapons
Weapons of mass destruction

War economies
Exogenous economic shocks
Wartime embargoes
Inner-directed economy
Market-oriented economic
  reform

QUESTIONS AND APPLICATION

1. One can break down the future of North Korea into three broad scenarios of change. List and discuss them in some detail.

2. Consider a possible North Korean attack of the South.

3. Give two reasons why a North Korean attack of South Korea is an unlikely scenario?

4. Under what circumstances do you think a North Korean attack of South Korea will become a viable option for North Korea?

5. Is such an attack preventable?

6. What are the three sets of economic problems that might cause North Korea to collapse?

7. North Korea has remarkably survived all political odds despite the downfall of the communist bloc and severe economic hardships causing a great famine. Are the recent reforms in this country sufficient to carry the regime through or is North Korea's collapse imminent?

8. In your opinion, which is the best possible outcome for North Korea? For South Korea? And for the international community at large? Which is the best overall outcome?

References

Choe, Sang T., and Kelly D. Huff. "North Korea in Transition: Time to Invest or Observe?" *Journal of Global Competitiveness*, Vol. 9, Issue 1, 2001, pp. 291–298.

Clifford, Mark. "How Much Longer, Kim Jong Il?" *China Journal*, July 18, 2002.

French, Howard W. "North Korea Adding a Pinch of Capitalism to Its Economy." *New York Times*, August 9, 2002.

Harrison, Selig S. *Korean Endgame.* Princeton, N.J.: Princeton University Press, 2002.

Jeon, Kyongmann. "The Likelihood and Implications of a North Korean Attack on the South." In Marcus Noland, ed., *Economic Integration of Korean Peninsula.* Washington, D.C.: Institute for International Economics, 1998, pp. 9–25.

Noland, Marcus, ed. *Economic Integration of Korean Peninsula.* Washington, D.C.: Institute for International Economics, 1998.

_____. "The North Korean Economy." *Economic and Regional Cooperation in Northeast Asia, Joint U.S.–Korea Academic Studies.* Washington, D.C.: Korean Economic Institute of America, 1996, pp. 148–149.

_____. Why North Korea Will Muddle Through." *Foreign Affairs*, July/August 1997, pp. 105–118.

_____, Sherman Robinson, and Tao Wang. "Famine in North Korea: Causes and Cures." *Economic Development and Cultural Change*, July 2001, pp. 741–767.

Oh, Kongdan, and Ralph C. Hassig. *North Korea Through the Looking Glass.* Washington, D.C.: Brookings Institution Press, 2000.

_____, and _____. "North Korea Between Collapse and Reform." *Asian Survey*, March/April 1999, pp. 287–309.

PART III

The North Korean Economy and Its Open Door Policy

Part III explains four closely related issues. First, it describes why North Korea suffered from negative economic growth for nine consecutive years in the 1990s, compelling Pyongyang to adopt an open door economic policy. Second, it discusses improved inter–Korean economic relations. Third, it discusses reasons to do business with North Korea, entry modes to North Korean markets, practical considerations in doing business with North Korea, and political risk analysis. Finally, it analyzes the North Korean famine and humanitarian relief programs.

5 The North Korean Economy

SUMMARY

In the first years following the Korean War (1950–1953), the centrally directed economy of North Korea had been larger in per capita income and had grown more rapidly than the more loosely controlled economy of South Korea. However, in the absence of rational and strategic economic planning, these advantages soon reached their limits. By the mid–1970s, South Korea's two successful five-year economic plans put the country ahead of North Korea. Loss of allies in the early 1990s, consecutive floods in 1995 and 1996, and a severe drought in 1997 caused the North Korean economy to shrink in the 1990s. Thus, while North Korea had gradually reformed its troubled economic system since the early 1990s, these measures were different from market-oriented reform. However, in July 2002, North Korea began to introduce the most significant liberalization measures since the start of communist rule in 1948 (French, 2002). This chapter examines a number of important North Korean economic issues, such as the North Korean famine, inter–Korean economic cooperation,

77

the North Korean legal system and foreign business cooperation, and the case for an economic policy of engagement with North Korea.

Introduction

North Korea, one of the world's poorest, most isolated
economies, faces desperate economic conditions. Industrial capital
stock is nearly beyond repair due to years of underinvestment and
spare-part shortages. In 2003, the nation faced its 10th year of food
shortages resulting from weather-related problems and chronic
shortages of fertilizer and fuel. Massive international food aid deliveries have allowed the regime to escape catastrophic economic failure resulting in mass starvation. Still, the population remains
vulnerable to prolonged malnutrition and deteriorating living conditions. Large-scale military spending eats up resources needed for
expanding investment and creating consumable goods. In the last
few years, the regime has placed a strong emphasis on expanding
foreign trade links, embracing modern technology, and attracting
foreign investment, but made no efforts toward relinquishing central control of national assets or undertaking Western-style market-
oriented reforms.

A general knowledge of the historical context is crucial to
understanding North Korea's situation today. After World War II,
Korea was split into a northern, communist half and a southern,
Western-oriented half. Kim Jong Il has held power since his father
(and the country's founder), President Kim Il Sung, died in 1994.
After decades of political and economic mismanagement, the North
relies heavily on international aid to feed its people, while continuing to expend resources to maintain an army of 1.1 million troops.
Today, North Korea's long-range missile development and research
into nuclear and chemical weapons are of major concern to the
international community.

In the first years, following the Korean War (1950–1953), the centrally directed economy of North Korea had grown more rapidly than the more loosely controlled economy of South Korea. North Korea opted for an inner-directed economy, which was centered on building its heavy industry at home while shying away from commitments abroad. Part of the reason for the short-term economic success of such a policy was that North Korea emphasized mass mobilization and used non-economic incentives to motivate workers—which proved very effective in the early years. Additionally, early economic success had been artificially inflated by massive economic aid and technical assistance from China and Russia (Christenson, 2000). However, in the absence of rational and strategic economic planning, these advantages soon reached their limits.

The following pages will address a number of practical issues relating to the North Korean economy today, such as the North Korean famine, inter–Korean economic cooperation, the North Korean legal system and foreign business cooperation, and the case for an economic policy of engagement with North Korea.

THE NORTH KOREAN FAMINE

No one knows for sure how many North Koreans died from the food shortages in the 1990s because North Korea is a police state that restricts or prohibits access for reporters and relief workers. However, international aid organizations estimate that the number of premature deaths from food shortages and related diseases ranged from 1,000,000 to 3,000,000 in the 1990s (Oh and Hassig, 1999).

This is as severe as the greatest famine in modern history. The Ethiopian famine led to the deaths of 1,000,000 people in that nation during 1984 and 1985 (Noland, Robinson, and Wang, 2001). In September 1995, North Korea, in a rare admission of vulnerability, appealed for help to the food agency of the United Nations (the World Food Program) and to donor countries. The most controversial question about the North Korean famine of 1995–1999 is not, "Who or what caused it?" but rather, "Who failed to stop it?" (Natsios, 2001). South Korea, Japan, China and Russia could have done much more to help their impoverished neighbor. American policy-makers initially denied the existence of the North Korean famine and then responded inadequately. For the most part, however, Natsios criticizes humanitarian aid officials and agencies that failed to act upon clear evidence of starvation that even the obsessively secretive North Korean regime could not entirely disguise.

Predictably, the North Korean economy began to contract as the collapse of the socialist bloc in 1990 deprived the nation of major markets. Because North Korea issues no consistent macroeconomic statistics, it is impossible to gain an accurate picture of its economy. Nevertheless, the Bank of Korea estimates that the gross national product (GNP) of North Korea fell from $23.1 billion in 1990 to $12.6 billion in 1998—a decline of 55 percent. Its foreign trade declined by 70 percent as the country's economy contracted and trade relations with former communist countries dwindled. In 1998, the country's foreign debt, in default since the 1980s, amounted to $12 billion—not a large figure for most countries, but equal to 96 percent of this country's GNP. North Korean factories are estimated to have operated at no more than 25 percent of capacity in the 1990s (Oh and Hassig, 2000). The health care system virtually ceased to operate; the food shortage became the most pressing economic problem.

Floods in 1995 and 1996 were followed by a severe drought in 1997 that reduced corn production by 50 percent. The contraction of the North Korean economy, combined with these three natural disasters, contributed significantly to the famine (Natsios, 2001). Certainly, North Korea has long been its own worst enemy. It is a rogue state with one of the largest land armies in the world. It has a dismal history of making threats to annihilate South Korea, of continuing rhetorical attacks against the U.S., and of producing weapons of mass destruction. By 1995 North Korea was, with Cuba, one of two remaining communist countries that steadfastly refused to acknowledge the bankruptcy of the great socialist experiment that had begun with the Russian revolution of 1917. Some scholars argue that the reason no country with a democratic government has experienced a famine is due to two factors (Arnold, 1988): first, a democratic government will listen to its people because voters have the ballot box as a means of expressing their panic and anger; second, in a democratic system, a free press will publicize any national crisis, thus forcing the government to respond. North Korea had neither a free press nor a democratic system of governance to deal with its unfolding disaster.

Why did North Korea suffer from negative economic growth for almost 10 years? Although many explanations have been offered for this decline, the economic slowdown began with the collapse of the international cooperative network among socialist countries. Four reasons stand out: increasing import prices, declining demand through market contraction, changes in the payment system, and withdrawal of capital by Russia and China.

First, the destruction of the cooperative system among socialist countries abolished socialist-friendly prices, which usually ranged between one-fourth to one-third of regular market prices. Second, the breakdown of the cooperative network among socialist countries resulted in market contraction and a decrease in demand. Third, the payment system changed from a quasi-barter system to a hard-currency payment system. Finally, in the late 1980s, China and Russia stopped providing new loans and began demanding repayment of outstanding loans. Consequently, today North Korea suffers from shortages of foreign currency, grain, spare parts, oil, technology, and morale; poor product quality, living standards, and production facilities—all of which damage the nation's ability to compete in international markets.

While enjoying economic benefits from South Korean business firms, the North Korean economy finally turned around in 1999. The Bank of Korea estimates that the North Korean economy grew by 6.2 percent in 1999, 1.3 percent in 2000, 3.7 percent in 2001, and 1.2 percent in 2002, after experiencing nine years of successive negative growth. In particular, the North Korean grain output recorded gains and its import volume expanded rapidly during the last few years. In addition, the average operation ratio of several industrial facilities of North Korea increased from 46 percent in February 1997 to 77 percent in 2001 (Lee, 2002).

III. THE NORTH KOREAN ECONOMY

In recent years, the Hyundai Group of South Korea has paid somewhere between $150 to $200 million per year for the Mt. Kumgang tourism project. China and Russia have increased their economic assistance to North Korea. Humanitarian assistance from the U.S., Japan, and other countries has increased as well. All of these factors have contributed to North Korea's economic growth in the past few years. North Korea, however, does not have sufficient production capacity to accommodate domestic consumption and to compensate for capital depreciation. Consequently, the recent positive economic growth in North Korea is vulnerable and could evaporate at any time.

In light of North Korea's culpability for its own economic woes, why should developed countries and humanitarian agencies bear any responsibility for the terrible North Korean famine, and why should they revise their behavior in similar situations in the future? The North Korean famine was greatly exacerbated by the fact that donor countries and humanitarian agencies responded to pressure from a powerful chorus of interest groups and politicians. These groups demanded that no food aid be provided until North Korea agreed to behave more responsibly on the international stage and until the regime could demonstrate that the aid would not be diverted from starving citizens to its military. In view of the famine's catastrophic effects, it seems clear that no nation or agency should have allowed political or strategic considerations to supersede the moral obligation to feed the hungry.

It is in the interest of the U.S. and South Korea to contribute even more generously in the future. In addition to the moral and ethical issues, practical considerations are paramount. Politicizing a famine to advance a diplomatic agenda is reprehensible, and it does a great disservice to the cause of peace in the region. Famines are destructive events with unpredictable, long-term consequences. Even if policy makers are unmoved by the ethical considerations of using mass starvation to force any nation to negotiate, they should be concerned about the profoundly destabilizing effects of famines. In recent years, hungry North Korean families have increasingly escaped across the border into China and South Korea; far more could follow. What will the South Koreans and the Chinese do to handle such an influx of refugees? In addition, if a famine initiates a chain of explosive events, the U.S. diplomacy may put the 37,000 American troops in South Korea at risk.

INTER-KOREAN ECONOMIC COOPERATION UNDER THE SUNSHINE POLICY

North Korea's approach to inter–Korean affairs had been deeply animated by the regime's own interpretation of unification: the two nations could be reunited only on North Korean terms. For its part, South Korea's approach to commerce with the North had also been governed and distorted by political considerations. Furthermore, three days after the beginning of the Korean War on June 25, 1950, the U.S. Congress approved legislation to ban all American exports to North Korea. Over the next four decades, U.S. legal sanctions concerning commercial and financial transactions steadily expanded to include 10 separate American laws by the early 1990s. With the signing of the U.S.–North Korean "Agreed Framework" on October 21, 1994, however, America formally embraced a new approach toward economic relations with North Korea, an approach that envisioned not only a progressive expansion of bilateral trade, but also de facto commitment of direct official aid from Washington to Pyongyang (Eberstadt, 1999).

As part of the new policy of engagement, the South Korean government announced a departure from its former approach in early 1998 and separated business from politics. Upon taking office in February 1998, South Korea's Kim Dae Jung and his government adopted a sunshine policy of engagement toward the North (Kim, 2000). The purpose of this policy was to legally allow individuals, organizations and even the government to provide aid to North Korea in spite of Pyongyang's hostility toward the government in Seoul. In other words, the sunshine policy was designed to separate humanitarian and business issues from political ones. This form of engagement was seen as the most promising choice for catalyzing change in North Korea and reducing its threats. This sunshine policy is based on three principles: South Korea will not tolerate any armed provocation from the North; it will not seek to absorb North Korea; and it will make every effort to promote reconciliation and cooperation with the North.

In September 1999, the U.S. eased its economic sanctions against North Korea for the first time in 50 years. The leaders of capitalist South Korea and communist North Korea met in Pyongyang on June 13, 2000, for the first time since the establishment of two separate governments in 1948—just three years after Korea's liberation from Japanese colonial rule. At the June 2000 meeting, the two nations' leaders agreed in principle to reduce tension on the Korean peninsula and to increase economic, social, and cultural exchanges. Even before the move to reconciliation, trade between the North and the South had steadily increased from $38 million in 1989 to $577 million in 2000. Moreover, South Korea has been the North's third largest trading partner since 1995 (Hong, 2001). The South's sunshine policy has further motivated North Korea to demonstrate a long-term commitment to inter–Korean economic cooperation.

Prior to the June 2000 summit meeting, agricultural-fishery products and processing-on-commission (POC) trade in textiles had accounted for most of North Korea's exports to the South. The POC trade had mainly consisted of simple products assembled by North Korean workers. Most of South Korea's exports to the North had consisted of non-business transactions, such as economic aid and goods related to the light water reactor project and the Mt. Kumgang tourism project. In addition, inter–Korean investment was very limited. Although about 40 South Korean companies had received permission to establish partnership arrangements with North Korea, most ventures were still in the planning stages and were not expected to make any profit for quite some time (Hong, 2000).

Many positive changes have taken place in North-South Korean relations since the historic 2000 summit talks. The most visible outcome of the new policy has been North Korea's cooperation with Hyundai Group for the development of the Mt. Kumgang tourism project. Both sides also agreed to re-link the severed South-North railway and build a new highway to link the South to Kaesong City just north of the demilitarized zone. In addition to these two projects, large-scale projects include the light water reactor project, Samsung's electronics complex and software joint development projects, and the auto repair and assembly factory of Pyung Hwa Motors. Other attempts, successful and unsuccessful, have been made to advance progress on such issues as divided family exchange reunions, the cancellation of U.S.–South Korean military exercises, economic assistance, drafts of agreements on investment protection, double taxation avoidance, and business dispute arbitration. Former President Kim Dae Jung received a Nobel Peace Prize in 2001 in recognition of the sunshine policy and other contributions. With many inter–Korean projects, both public and private, already contracted and under way since the June 2000 summit meeting, North-South commerce would seem poised not only to continue, but also to expand significantly in the years ahead.

By increasing inter–Korean commercial contacts—through trade, joint ventures, technology transfer arrangements, infrastructure development projects, and other initiatives—it will be possible to diminish tensions in the Korean peninsula as well as to accelerate North Korean internal reform. Proponents of such an approach make four independent but interrelated arguments for their case (Eberstadt, 1999). First, the North Korean system is in desperate need of precisely the advantages that inter–Korean economic cooperation can provide. Second, North Korean leadership understands the country's economic difficulties and the urgency with which trade opportunities and other international economic contacts must now be pursued. Third, an economic opening in North Korea would be in South Korea's own financial interest, rather than simply an exercise in checkbook diplomacy. Fourth, South Korea has a record of demonstrated success in bringing formerly hostile communist countries to the point of rapprochement through economic diplomacy.

A foundation for expanding inter–Korean economic cooperation has been created since the June 2000 summit meeting. It will be successful if North and South Korea work under the principles of mutual and balanced development. The speed and scope of economic cooperation will depend on such factors as North Korea's attitude toward reform and the opening of its economy, the fundraising ability of the South Korean government and its corporations, and the cooperation and participation of the international community.

NORTH KOREA'S LEGAL SYSTEM AND FOREIGN BUSINESS COOPERATION

Under the custodianship of Kim Il Sung and Kim Jong Il, *juche* (the principle of self-reliance) has guided North Korea's ideology. North Korea's economy aspires to the ideological principle of *juche* under the following three governing and economic principles. First, North Korea's constitution stipulates that solely the state and cooperative organizations own all means of production. Therefore, industrial facilities and commercial enterprises are state-owned. Most farms operate as collectives under the strict guidance of the party. The second principle is centralization of all economic planning. The state formulates unified and detailed plans to guarantee a high rate of production growth and balanced development of the national economy. The third principle of *juche* is self-sufficiency. Socialist production relations are based on the foundation of an independent and comprehensive national economy. In accordance with *juche*, North Korea's foreign trade amounts only to around 10 percent of its gross national product (GNP)—far below that of most other nations.

The recent economic crisis, however, forced North Korea to seriously consider the future of its autarkic system, resulting in a host of new laws addressing foreign investment, relations with capitalist firms, and new zones of free trade. North Korea promulgated many internal banking, labor, and investment laws. The government recognized the numerous potential benefits of expanded economic cooperation with South Korea and other countries. Direct benefits included creation of infrastructure and facilities, employee wages paid by South Korea or foreign companies, sale of raw materials, and development of related industries and neighboring areas. Indirect benefits included attraction of foreign capital, improved national risk ratings, and the easing of economic sanctions by the U.S. and its allies.

North Korea has developed a legal framework for foreign business cooperation since it initiated its open-door policy in the early 1990s. For example, the New Socialist Constitution of 1998 and subsequent amendments include three basic laws designed to establish a framework for external economic cooperation: the Foreign Equity Law, the Contractual Joint Venture Law, and the Foreign Enterprises Law (Lee, 2000). Such laws demonstrate North Korea's recognition that any country wishing to attract foreign investment must adopt laws that define property, govern contracts, stipulate taxes, and in other ways make economic development predictable enough for foreign firms to comfortably participate.

The Foreign Equity Law governs the rights and obligations for establishing and managing joint ventures on North Korean soil. This law confines the geographic region available for such equity joint ventures to two free economic zones: a Free Economic and Trade Zone of the Rajin-Sonbong region established in 1991 and a Special Administrative Zone of Shinujiu established in 2002. Some ventures may be established in other regions, if necessary, but this may prove difficult for foreign companies. The law further opens doors to South Korean investors with a provision that includes "Koreans living outside the territory of North Korea," while the old law confined such investors to only "the Korean traders and manufacturers in Japan." North Korea prefers investments that involve internationally competitive products, infrastructure development, or scientific research and technological development.

The Contractual Joint Venture Law governs the rights and obligations of concerned parties for establishing and managing a contractual joint venture. One major purpose of this law is to expand economic cooperation and technological exchange between North Korea and the rest of the world. North Korea prefers to establish contractual joint ventures primarily in sectors producing exportable goods using advanced technology, and in the tourism and service sectors. Like equity joint ventures, the main regional scopes available for contractual joint ventures are the two free economic zones mentioned above, though such ventures could be expanded elsewhere within the territory of North Korea.

The Foreign Enterprises Law provides the basic rules for the creation of wholly foreign-owned enterprises. The law provides all relevant guidelines for the business activities of foreign enterprises. According to this law, foreign enterprises must carry out their business activities according to the charter and by-laws of enterprise management, which are subject to approval by the North Korean government.

In addition to the laws governing these three forms of foreign investment, North Korea has continued to issue a series of detailed laws and regulations necessary for attracting foreign investments. They include laws concerning the following: Taxes on Foreign Invested Enterprise and Foreigners, Foreign Exchange Control, Foreign-Invested Banks, the Leasing of Land, and Customs Duties. These laws and other economic reforms undertaken by North Korea indicate that the country is serious about stabilizing its domestic economy and improving its living standards. In promoting economic advancement, foreign trade and external economic cooperation have received top priority because North Korea recognizes that economic expansion leads to increased demand for foreign currency.

The current regime under Kim Jong Il has adopted an open-door policy to overcome the political and economic difficulties that have plagued the nation since 1994. A series of new laws and regulations related to the nation's movement toward a more open economy have the following characteristics: First, North Korea has recently established the two free economic zones in a bid to attract foreign investments. Second, the government's control over foreign investment has been strengthened. Third, the scope of foreign-investment enterprises has been expanded. Fourth, investment by overseas Koreans has been separated from that of other foreign investors. Under this particular regulation, the investment of overseas Koreans is expected to increase sharply.

Regardless of the eventual outcome and practical implications of such regulatory changes, the legislation over the last couple of years has accelerated North Korea's efforts to attract foreign capital and open its doors to foreign investment. Although U.S. economic sanctions were eased in 1999, North Korea has still failed to attract any significant capital flow, partially due to the Bush administration's hard-line stand against North Korea. In view of the benefits of full North Korean participation in the international community, the Great Powers, particularly the U.S., should work toward building diplomatic and economic ties with North Korea. Such ties will encourage the country to continue developing its open door policy.

THE CASE FOR AN ECONOMIC POLICY OF ENGAGEMENT WITH NORTH KOREA

At the end of the Korean War in 1953, the U.S. adopted a general policy of military containment, diplomatic isolation, and economic sanctions against North Korea, while maintaining ties with South Korea. However, a series of events since the late 1980s transformed the relations between the two Koreas from confrontation to reconciliation. One of the most critical factors in this transformation was an emerging openness in the American attitude toward North Korea. South Korea's Kim Dae Jung's sunshine policy enjoyed an unprecedented honeymoon period with the Clinton administration. While the Geneva Agreed Framework in 1994 defused the potential nuclear crisis in Korea, the Perry process—a process of close consultation with South Korea and Japan recommended by former U.S. Defense Secretary William Perry—was instrumental in facilitating the sunshine policy. However, the new hard-line direction of the George W. Bush administration contributed to the deterioration of inter–Korean relations.

Relations between the U.S. and North Korea had reached a high point in the final months of the Clinton administration. That trend culminated in a visit to Pyongyang by then Secretary of State Madeleine Albright, the highest-level U.S. official to travel to the North. Her visit came just a few weeks after a top North Korean official visited President Clinton in the White House in October 2000. These and other events transformed relations among the two Koreas and the surrounding powers from confrontation to engagement. Consequently, the four Pacific powers—China, Japan, Russia, and the U.S.—had significantly expanded the scope of their cooperation in military, diplomatic and economic fields for a while. South Korea had increased the level of cooperation with these four powers during the same period. Even North Korea gradually improved its relations with South Korea, Japan and the U.S. until George W. Bush took the oath of office as U.S. president on January 25, 2001, and made known his intention to revert to a tougher line on relations.

The Bush administration quickly put North Korean relations on hold until a policy review was conducted. By early July 2001, the new administration's policy, under the influence of Secretary of State Colin Powell, validated a continuation of the U.S.–North Korean dialogue that began during the Clinton era. However, North Korea expressed through other channels its strong concern that the Bush administration operated under a different and more difficult set of principles than the Clinton administration. Since then the relationship between the United States and North Korea has deteriorated from engagement to containment; from containment to confrontation; and from confrontation to crisis—first regional, then international.

In the past, the U.S. State Department had labeled North Korea, Iraq and Iran as "rogue states" whose military policy and support of other groups supposedly threatened Washington's security. In his State of the Union address on January 29, 2002, President Bush labeled these three countries as the "axis of evil," thus extending his war on terrorism. This label is one of the harshest used by the U.S. administration to describe North Korea. Furthermore, according to Bush, "North Korea is a regime arming with missiles and weapons of mass destruction, while starving its citizens." Bush's comments are emblematic of his determination to take a hard line on dealing with North Korea, a distinct shift from the Clinton-era policy of engagement to a new U.S. policy of containment. As expected, a U.S. policy shift from engagement to containment toward North Korea reinforced the North Korean belief that it should develop weapons of mass destruction for its own survival.

From October 3 to October 5, 2002, the U.S. and North Korea had their first high-level contact in Pyongyang after a nearly two-year hiatus, but they failed to reach any agreement on a range of security issues. In fact, this brief interaction effectively worsened U.S.–North Korean relations. North Korea charged that James Kelly, U.S. Assistant Secretary of State for East Asian and Pacific Affairs, visited North Korea not to negotiate but to make the following demands: the suspension of nuclear weapons program, verifiable controls on missile production and exports, the reduction of conventional forces along the 38th parallel, and the improvement of human rights. To the Bush administration's surprise, North Korean officials admitted to Kelly that his evidence about their secret nuclear weapons program was correct. The North's admission of these actions violates the 1994 Agreed Framework, in which it pledged to abandon its nuclear weapons program in return for the construction of two light-water reactors and 500,000 tons of fuel oil each year until the reactors were completed.

North Korea offered talks with the U.S. to rectify the concerns over its nuclear weapons program. However, the Bush administration rejected these proposals, which were actually similar to North Korea's repeated offers over the last 50 years to give up its nuclear weapons program in exchange for a nonaggression pact with the U.S. In addition, Japan, South Korea, and the European Union agreed that oil deliveries to North Korea should continue, as it represented the best available bait to lure the nation away from developing weapons of mass destruction. However, on November 14, 2002, the executive board of the Korean Energy Development Organization (KEDO) decided to end their monthly fuel deliveries to North Korea under heavy pressure from the Bush administration. In late December 2002, North Korea evicted international nuclear inspectors in a move to restart its main nuclear weapon complex, which experts believe could produce several powerful nuclear weapons within months.

Former South Korean President Kim's sunshine policy was centered on the concept that North Korea's threats arose from insecurity. Abandoned by its old patrons, economically bankrupt, politically isolated, and starving, North Korea saw the pursuit of nuclear weapons and ballistic missiles as its only path to security and survival. South Korea's policy of engagement was designed to reduce this insecurity and end the proliferation of threats. Various incentives such as economic aid, normalized relations, and reduced security tensions were provided to give North Korea a stake in the status quo and persuade North Korean leaders that they could best serve their interests by discontinuing the development of weapons of mass destruction (Cha, 2002). South Korean president, Roh Moo Hyun, supports his predecessor's sunshine policy of engagement with North Korea. Both leaders believe that dialogue is the only way to resolve the North's nuclear issue peacefully.

As an extension of this policy, continued engagement and humanitarian aid today can achieve the same two goals that the Bush administration seeks to achieve through its hard-line policy. Hard-liners have traditionally felt that confrontation and containment would force North Korea to collapse or concede to foreign demands. This thinking has proven to be dangerously incorrect and has contributed to the further destabilization of relations with North Korea. In contrast, engagement and aid together can hasten the demise of the anachronistic elements of the North Korean regime. While direct aid alone may seem to improve the North Korean situation in the short term, it can also create a dangerous "spiral of expectations" among North Korean citizens. This makes engagement even more essential. Humanitarian aid combined with engagement can help prepare for Korean unification by winning over the hearts and minds of the North Korean people. Most North Korean experts agree that an effective solution would be a U.S. promise to normalize relations and cooperate with North Korea's reform efforts if North Korea agrees to undertake a verified and permanent abandonment of the weapons programs (Shirk, 2002).

An induced collapse of North Korea through policies of containment, if successful, would bring insurmountable problems to South Korea. To absorb some 22 million people whose living standards are less than one-eighteenth those of South Korean citizens could cost many billions of dollars. Equally serious would be the political impact of bringing into South Korea's fragile democracy a people who had only known Stalinist politics and the worship of the Great Leader Kim Il Sung. Another serious problem concerns possible social chaos from a massive migration of Northerners into the already overpopulated South.

If North Korea faces political and economic problems beyond its control due to the U.S. containment policy, there is a distinct possibility that North Korea could invade South Korea out of desperation. In fact, North Korea has repeatedly stated that it will not capitulate without bringing South Korea into a conflict. Seoul's location just 25 miles south of the demilitarized zone makes it virtually impossible to protect from unprovoked artillery attacks. Even with modern anti-battery guided weapons, the greater Seoul metropolitan area could not escape damage that would wreak havoc in the area where about a third of South Korea's population makes its living.

Some analysts argue that North Korea's recent policy directions indicate substantive internal reform and external engagement. The greatest contribution that the U.S. could make toward durable peace and stability on the Korean peninsula would be to normalize economic and diplomatic relations with North Korea and enter into an extensive program of engagement. Strategic, responsible engagement with the North will create fissures within isolationist North Korean policies and hasten internal change in desirable directions. The long-term result will be to welcome North Korea into productive, sustainable membership in the international economic and diplomatic community.

KEY TERMS AND CONCEPTS

North Korean famine
Centrally directed economy
Market contraction
Quasi-barter system
Hard-currency payment system
Negative growth
Inter-Korean cooperation
Economic sanctions against
   North Korea

Processing-on-commission
   (POC)
Divided family exchange
   reunions
Autarkic system
New Socialist Constitution
Foreign Equity Law
Contractual Joint Venture Law
Foreign Enterprises Law

QUESTIONS AND APPLICATION

1. What events contributed to the gravity of the North Korean famine?

2. How could the North Korean famine have been prevented?

3. How does a catastrophe such as the North Korean famine affect neighboring countries?

4. Give two historical examples of foreign policy towards North Korea that aggravated this country's economy. Did hard-line approaches used by the United States induce North Korea to improve its human rights record? Or did they induce North Korea to reconsider its nuclear program?

5. Which country initiated the most important step in engaging North Korea in international trade? What was the proposal? How has it affected the Korean peninsula to date?

6. What are the recent laws introduced or amended by North Korea about foreign trade? Explain each briefly. Which foreign policy is responsible for their formulation?

7. How do the recent economic laws introduced by North Korea contradict the principle of *juche*?

8. North Korea has admitted its violation of the Agreed

Framework of 1994. In your opinion, how should the international community react to this admission?

9. What do you believe would be the outcome of a continued and improved policy of economic engagement with North Korea? Many analysts have examined this issue. You may explain reasons why you agree or disagree by providing a critical and analytical support for your answer.

REFERENCES

Arnold, David. *Famine: Social Crisis and Change*. Oxford: Basil Blackwell, 1988.

Bracken, Paul. *Fire in the East*. New York: Perennial, 1999.

Breen, Michael. *The Koreans*. New York: St. Martin's Press, 1998.

Buss, Claude A. *The United States and the Republic of Korea: Background for Policy*. Stanford, California: Hoover International Studies, Hoover Institution Press, Stanford University, 1988.

Cha, Victor D. "Korea's Place in the Axis." Foreign Affairs, May/June 2002, pp. 79–92.

_____. "The Rationale for Enhanced Engagement of North Korea." *Asian Survey*, November/December 1999, pp. 845–866.

Christenson, Richard A. "North Korea's Economic Development: An Agenda for Cooperation." In The Korea Economic Institute of America, *The Political Economy of Korean Reconciliation and Reform*, 2000, pp. 51–58.

Cummings, Bruce. *Korea's Place in the Sun*. New York: W.W. Norton, 1997.

Eberstadt, Nicholas. "Disparities in Socioeconomic Development in Divided Korea." *Asian Survey*, November/December 2000, pp. 867–893.

Fox News. "North Korea Security Talk Pulled Off Table." www.foxnews.com, July 2, 2002.

French, Howard W. "North Korea Adding a Pinch of Capitalism to Its Economy." *New York Times*, August 9, 2002, p. A1.

Harrison, Selig S. "Time to Leave Korea?" *Foreign Affairs*, March/April, 2001, pp. 62–78.

III. The North Korean Economy

Harvey, Joe. "N. Korea Hits Back at Bush's Evil Tag." www.CNN.com/WORLD, February 1, 2002.

Hong, Soon-jick. "North-South Economic Cooperation." In The Korea Economic Institute of America, ed., *Korea's Economy 2001*, Vol 17. Washington, D.C.: KEI, 2001, pp. 77–81.

Kim Dae Jung. "Reconcile, Cooperate, and Live in Peaceful Coexistence." *Presidents and Prime Ministers*, November/December 2000, pp. 22–24.

Korea Economic Institute of America, ed. *The Political Economy of Korean Reconciliation and Reform.* Washington, D.C.: KEI, 2001.

Korean Overseas Information Service. *Focus on Korea: This Is Korea.* Seoul: Seoul International Publishing House, 1986.

Lee, Doowon. "The Economic Outlook for Reconciliation and Reunification." In Kongdan Oh and Ralph Hassig, *Korea Briefing.* New York: M.E. Sharpe, 2002, pp. 43–76.

Lee, Eric. "Development of North Korea's Legal Regime Governing Foreign Business Cooperation: A Revisit under the New Socialist Constitution of 1998." *Northwestern Journal of International Law & Business*, Fall 2000, pp. 199–242.

Mazarr, Michael J. "Predator States and War: The North Korea Case." In Dong Whan Park, ed., *The United States and Two Koreas: A New Triangle.* Boulder: Lynne Rienner Publishers, 1998, pp. 75–96.

Natsios, Andrew S. *The Great North Korean Famine.* Washington, D.C.: The United States Institute of Peace Press, 2001.

Noland, Marcus. "Why North Korea Will Muddle Through." *Foreign Affairs*, July/August 1997, 105–117.

_____, ed. *Economic Integration of the Korean Peninsula.* Washington, D.C.: Institute for International Economics, January 1998.

_____, Sherman Robinson, and Tao Wang. "Famine in North Korea: Causes and Cures." *Economic Development and Cultural Change*, July 2001, pp. 741–767.

Oberdorfer, Don. *The Two Koreas*, New York: Basic Books, 1997.

Oh, Kongdan, and Ralph C. Hassig. *North Korea Through the Looking Glass.* Washington, D.C.: Brookings Institution Press, 2000.

_____, and _____. "North Korea Between Collapse and Reform." *Asian Survey*, March/April 1999, pp. 287–309.

Olson, Edward A. "U.S. Security Policy and the Two Koreas." *World Affairs*, Spring 2000, pp. 150–157.

Park, Dong Whan, ed. *The U.S. and the Two Koreas.* Boulder: Lynne Rienner Publishers, 1988.

Park, Philip. "The Future of the Democratic People's Republic of Korea." *Journal of Contemporary Asia.* Vol. 31, No. 1, 2000, pp. 104–120.

Rubin, Michael. "Don't Engage Rogue Regimes." *The Wall Street Journal,* December 12, 2001, p. A18.

Shirk, Susan. "A New North Korea." *Washington Post,* October 22, 2002, p. A27.

Slavin, Barbara. "Critics Question Tough Talk on Iran, North Korea." *USA Today,* January 31, 2002, p. 8A.

_____, and Laurence McQuillan. "Axis of Evil Scoffs at Speech." *USA Today,* January 31, 2002, p. 1A.

USA Today. "Bush Team Defends U.S. Nuke Plans." www.usatoday.com, March 10, 2002.

6 Inter-Korean Economic Relations

SUMMARY

For the past five decades, North Korea's approach to inter–Korean affairs has been deeply animated by the regime's own interpretation of unification: The two nations could be reunited only on North Korean terms. For its part, South Korea's approach to commerce with the North has also been governed and distorted by political considerations. At the same time, the U.S. has played an important role in inter–Korean affairs. Three days after the beginning of the Korean War on June 25, 1950, the U.S. Congress approved legislation to ban all American exports to North Korea. Over the next four decades, U.S. legal sanctions concerning commercial and financial transactions steadily expanded to include 10 separate American laws by the early 1990s. With the signing of the U.S.–North Korean "Agreed Framework" on October 21, 1994, however, America formally embraced a new approach toward economic relations with North Korea: an approach that envisioned not only a progressive expansion of bilateral trade, but also de facto commitment of direct official aid from Washington to

Pyongyang (Eberstadt, 1999). A policy of engagement with North Korea adopted in 1998 by South Korea stimulated inter–Korean economic cooperation even further. This chapter discusses a comparative economic analysis of the two Koreas, inter–Korean trade, inter–Korean investment, and suggestions for improvement of inter–Korean economic relations.

SOUTH KOREA'S NEW POLICY OF ENGAGEMENT

In early 1998, the South Korean government announced a departure from its former approach as part of its new policy of engagement, to separate business from politics. South Korea's President Kim Dae Jung adopted a sunshine policy of engagement toward the North after taking office in February 1998 (Kim, 2000). The purpose of this policy was to legally allow individuals, organizations, and even the government to provide aid to North Korea in spite of Pyongyang's hostility toward the government in Seoul. The sunshine policy was designed to separate humanitarian and business issues from political ones. This form of engagement was seen as the most promising choice for catalyzing change in North Korea and reducing its threats. This sunshine policy is based on three complementary principles: South Korea will not tolerate any armed provocation from the North; it will not seek to absorb North Korea; and it will make every effort to promote reconciliation and cooperation with the North.

In September 1999, the U.S. eased its economic sanctions against North Korea for the first time in 50 years. The leaders of capitalist South Korea and communist North Korea met in Pyongyang on June 13, 2000, for the first time since the establishment of two separate governments in 1948—which had happened just three years after Korea's liberation from Japanese colonial rule. At the June 2000 meeting, the two nations' leaders agreed in principle to reduce tension on the Korean peninsula and to increase economic, social, and cultural exchanges. Even before the move toward reconciliation, trade between the North and the South had steadily increased from $38 million in 1989 to $577 million in 2000. Moreover, South Korea has been the North's third-largest trading partner since 1995 (Hong, 2001). The South's sunshine policy has further motivated North Korea to demonstrate a long-term commitment to inter–Korean economic cooperation.

A COMPARATIVE ECONOMIC ANALYSIS OF NORTH AND SOUTH KOREA

The per capita income of North Korea was larger than that of South Korea from 1948 until 1970. Furthermore, the gross national product (GNP) of North Korea increased from $1.53 billion in 1960 to $9.4 billion in 1975, a 6.2-fold increase. During this 15-year period, North Korea's GNP grew at an average compound rate of 13 percent per year. During the next 15 years, from 1975 to 1990, its GNP grew more slowly, at an average compound rate of 6 percent per year. Although these growth rates for North Korea were lower than those for South Korea, they represented very respectable numbers at the time. It is important to remember that after the Korean War, the Western world adopted a general policy of military containment, diplomatic isolation, and economic sanctions against North Korea.

North Korea's per capita personal income remained higher than South Korea's during this early period (1950–1974). There were a number of reasons for this. First, North Korea possessed extensive economic resources to build a modern economy. North Korea had 43 sizable varieties of mineral deposits and nonferrous metals that were non-existent or less available in South Korea. North Korea's natural environment is also highly conducive to economic development. Three major rivers—Yalu, Tuman, and Taedong—supplement efficient means of coal transportation and power supply. Major ports—Chungjin, Kimchaek, Hungnam, Wonsan, Nampo, and Shinuiju—service the coastlines.

III. The North Korean Economy

Second, North Korea inherited the basic infrastructure of a modern economy because of Japan's substantial investment in development during the Japanese occupation (Savada, 1993). While the southern half of Korea produced mostly rice and had only light industry such as textiles, the Japanese had developed heavy industry in the northern half of Korea, including the metal and chemical industries, hydroelectric power, and mining. Third, North Korea opted for an inner-directed economy, which was centered on building its heavy industries at home while avoiding commitments abroad. Part of the reason for the short-term economic success of such a policy was that North Korea emphasized mass mobilization and used non-economic incentives to spur workers. These proved very effective in the early years. Early economic success also owed much to massive economic aid and technical help from China and Russia.

The tables began to turn in the 1970s. South Korea began to see the fruits of its two successive five-year economic plans driven by exports as the major growth engine. By 1975, the South Korean economy ($21 billion) had grown to be more than twice as large as the North Korean economy ($9 billion). Furthermore, the per capita income of South Korea ($594) had surpassed that of the North ($579) for the first time since the two Koreas were formed in 1948. By 1996, South Korea reached a per capita income of more than $10,000, enabling it to achieve the status of an advanced country. At the same time, North Korea had begun experiencing negative economic growth and chronic trade deficits in the early 1990s. Table 6.1 shows that today the South Korean economy in purchasing power parity is 39 times larger in gross national product and 18 times larger in per capita income than the North Korean economy.

Table 6.2 shows that North Korea suffered from negative economic growth for nine consecutive years from 1990 to 1998. Although many explanations have been offered for this decline, the economic slowdown began with the collapse of the international cooperative network among socialist countries. Four major reasons for the economic difficulties of North Korea stand out. First, in 1991 the Soviet Union underwent a political and ideological

6. INTER-KOREAN ECONOMIC RELATIONS

Table 6.1: Key Economic Statistics
of North and South Koreas

Variable	South Korea	North Korea	S Korea/N. Korea
Area	98,480 sq km	120,540 sq km	0.82 times
Population	48 million	22 million	2.18 times
Economic output	$865 billion	$22 billion	39.32 times
Per capita income	$18,000	$1,000	18.00 times
Exports	$168.3 billion	$0.708 billion	237.71 times
Imports	$152.3 billion	$1.686 billion	90 times

Source: *The World Factbook*, the Central Intelligence Agency of the United States, *www.cia.gov/*, February 3, 2003.

upheaval, which quickly led to its breakup into 15 independent countries. The Soviet Union, as a major political ally to North Korea, had been not only an important trading partner, but also a significant provider of economic assistance until the 1980s. In 1980, for example, the Soviet Union sold oil to North Korea at two-thirds of the world market price and provided $260 million of additional economic aid to the country. All of this support gradually dissipated, however. By the late 1980s, the Soviet Union and China stopped providing new loans to North Korea and began to demand repayments of outstanding loans. By 1990, the subsidized oil shipments, as well as the monetary aid from the Soviet Union to North Korea, had completely stopped (Noland, 1996).

Second, consecutive floods in 1995 and 1996 and a record drought in 1997 caused a massive loss of crops and cultivated land, further decimating the already anemic North Korean economy. Analysts estimate that 18 percent of North Korea's farmland was permanently destroyed by these disasters. Considering that 30 percent of the North Korean economy is agricultural, it is not difficult to imagine the magnitude of the impact on the lives of North Korea's citizens. The overall economic environment was so moribund that children were seen in the marketplace hunting for food left over from adult tables (Park, 1998).

Third, North Korea, with one of the largest land armies in the world, had built its economy mainly with heavy industry to sup-

III. The North Korean Economy

Table 6.2: Annual Economic Growth
Rates for North and South Koreas

Year	North Korea	South Korea	Year	North Korea	South Korea
1990	-3.70%	9.00%	1997	-6.30%	5.00%
1991	-3.50%	9.20%	1998	-1.10%	-6.70%
1992	-6.00%	5.40%	1999	6.20%	10.90%
1993	-4.20%	5.50%	2000	1.30%	9.30%
1994	-0.10%	8.30%	2001	3.70%	3.00%
1995	-4.10%	8.90%	2002	1.20%	6.00%
1996	-3.60%	6.80%			

Source: The Bank of Korea

port its military buildup, while largely neglecting consumer goods. Large-scale military spending absorbed resources needed for expanding investment and creating consumable goods. In fact, North Korea had allocated as much as 30 percent of its GNP to accomplish the four goals in military buildup: transforming the nation into a fortress, arming all the people of the country, training an elite military force, and modernizing military weapons. Consequently, North Koreans experienced shortages in housing, clothing, and food.

Finally, poor implementation of the rationing system and an uneven distribution of wealth caused the North Korean economy to contract. Rice and other necessities had been distributed bi-weekly, but a lack of efficient food allocation caused starvation for many, while some North Koreans enjoyed significant personal wealth (Kwon, 2002). The ineffective distribution system created two-tier pricing levels: the black market price and the official government price. To correct these problems, North Korea recently took new measures: large wage increases for workers and price increases for everything from food and electricity to housing. In June 2002, the country quietly stopped passing out rations to its 22 million citizens to bring price levels closer to realistic numbers (French, 2002).

INTER-KOREAN TRADE

Officially, South and North Korea do not recognize their trade as foreign trade per se; they treat the trade as domestic exchange. However, South Korea has emerged as the third-largest trading partner for North Korea since 1995. Furthermore, South Korea is not far behind Japan in terms of total trade volume with North Korea. Inter-Korean trade accounted for approximately 20 percent of North Korea's entire trade volume in 2002. This highlights the important role of inter–Korean trade for the North Korean economy.

As a rule, South Korean imports from North Korea have been primary products, such as metals and marine products. North Korean imports from South Korea have consisted mostly of chemical products, textile products, and goods from non-commercial transactions (Korea Herald, 2002). Although inter–Korean trade has reached its historic peak of more than $400 million in the last two years (see Table 6.3), the amount of commercial transactions between the two Koreas is expected to grow rather slowly in the coming years because of the lingering political and military instability in the region, the lack of a legal and institutional framework in North Korea, high transportation costs, poor North Korean infrastructure, lack of North Korean purchasing power and product variety, and difficulty in finding markets for North Korean products.

Inter-Korean trade began after South Korea adopted an open-door policy toward North Korea in July 1988. North and South Korea had a noticeable amount of trade for the first time in 1989. In spite of the short history of trade between the two Koreas, Table 6.3 shows two clear patterns. One of the most striking signs in inter–Korean trade is the increasing volume. The volume grew from $18.7 million in 1989 to $641.7 million in 2002, a 35-fold increase in just 13 years. The growth pattern was interrupted only a few times, mainly because of political squabbles over the Non-Proliferation Treaty (NPT), a North Korean agreement to abandon its nuclear weapons program ambitions.

III. The North Korean Economy

Table 6.3. North Korea's Inter-Korean Trade (in million US$)

Year	Exports to South	Imports from South	Total	Balance
1989	18.7	0.0	18.7	18.70
1990	12.2	1.2	13.4	11.00
1991	105.7	5.5	111.2	100.20
1992	162.8	10.6	173.4	152.20
1993	178.1	8.4	186.5	169.70
1994	176.3	18.2	194.5	158.10
1995	222.9	64.4	287.3	158.50
1996	182.4	69.6	252.0	112.80
1997	193.0	115.3	308.3	77.70
1998	92.3	129.6	221.9	(37.30)
1999	121.6	211.8	333.4	(90.20)
2000	152.4	272.7	425.1	(120.30)
2001	176.2	226.7	402.9	(50.50)
2002	271.6	370.1	641.7	(234.50)

Sources: The Ministry of Unification, the Republic of Korea.

With the Asian financial crisis in full bloom and the sharp contraction of the South Korean economy, inter–Korean trade in 1998 contracted 28 percent from its peak of $308 million in 1997. However, inter–Korean trade expanded 50 percent in 1999, mainly due to the rapid economic recovery of South Korea. Another contributing factor involved the South Korean government's initiatives to facilitate easier trade and investment with North Korea under the sunshine policy.

Another important economic pattern is the trade imbalance between the two Koreas. North Korea's exports consistently exceeded its imports by an appreciable margin from 1989 through 1997. North Korea enjoyed a trade surplus with South Korea due to a number of factors, such as North Korea's lack of hard currency with which to purchase South Korean goods, and the political sensitivity in North Korea over goods identifiably from South Korea. However, this trend reversed in 1998, mainly due to a substantial increase in non-commercial shipments from the South, including humanitarian aid, goods related to the Mt. Kumgang tourism project, and goods related to the construction of light water reactors.

INTER-KOREAN INVESTMENT

Under the custodianship of Kim Il Sung and Kim Jong Il, *juche* (the principle of self-reliance) has guided North Korea's ideology for many years. The recent economic crisis, however, forced North Korea to seriously consider the future of its autarkic system, resulting in a host of new laws addressing foreign investment, relations with capitalist firms, and new zones of free trade. North Korea promulgated many internal banking, labor, and investment laws. The government recognized the numerous potential benefits of expanded economic cooperation with South Korea and other countries. Direct benefits included creation of infrastructure and facilities, employee wages paid by South Korea or foreign companies, sale of raw materials, and development of related industries and neighboring areas. Indirect benefits included attraction of foreign capital, improved national risk ratings, and the easing of economic sanctions by the U.S. and its allies.

North Korea has developed a legal framework for foreign business cooperation since it initiated its open-door policy in the early 1990s. For example, the New Socialist Constitution of 1998 and subsequent amendments include three basic laws designed to establish a framework for external economic cooperation: the Foreign Equity Law, the Contractual Joint Venture Law, and the Foreign Enterprises Law (Lee, 2000).

In addition to these laws, North Korea has continued to issue a series of detailed regulations necessary for attracting additional foreign investment and participation in the North Korean economy. New laws include taxes on foreign invested enterprise and foreigners, foreign exchange control, foreign-invested banks, the leasing of land, and customs duties. The Foreign Trade Act of February 2001 and the Enforcement Decree of the Foreign Investment

Protection Act of December 2001 widen existing fissures in North Korea's anachronistic socialist constitutional faith. These laws and other economic reforms indicate that North Korea is serious about stabilizing its domestic economy and improving its living standards. They also demonstrate North Korea's recognition that any country wishing to attract foreign investment must adopt laws that define property, govern contracts, stipulate taxes, and in other ways make economic development predictable enough for foreign firms to comfortably participate. In promoting economic advancement, foreign trade and external economic cooperation have received top priority because North Korea recognizes that economic expansion leads to increased demand for foreign currency.

The current regime under Kim Jong Il has adopted an open-door policy to overcome the political and economic difficulties that have plagued the nation since 1994. The nation's movement toward a more open economy is demonstrated through various changes: First, North Korea has recently established two free economic zones in a bid to attract foreign investment. Second, the government's control over foreign investment has been strengthened. Third, the scope of foreign-investment enterprises has been expanded. Fourth, investment by overseas Koreans has been separated from that of other foreign investors. Under this particular regulation, the investment of overseas Koreans is expected to increase sharply.

Several positive changes have taken place in inter–Korean investment thanks to new North Korean laws and regulations, and the nation's open-door policy. The most visible outcome of the new policy has been North Korea's cooperation with Hyundai for the development of the Mt. Kumgang tourism project. Both sides also agreed to re-link the severed South-North railway and build a new highway to link the South to Kaesong City just north of the demilitarized zone. In addition to these two projects, large-scale projects include the light water reactor project, Samsung's electronics complex and software joint development projects, and the auto repair and assembly factory of Pyung Hwa Motors. Other attempts, successful and unsuccessful, have been made to advance progress on such issues as divided family exchange reunions, the cancellation of U.S.–South Korean military exercises, economic assistance, drafts of agreements on investment protection, double taxation avoidance, and business dispute arbitration.

In the conceivable future, inter–Korean investment is the most significant of the external investment possibilities for North Korea. Although North Korea has taken many measures to create a favorable environment for direct investment, there are still many hurdles to overcome before South Korea makes substantial additional investments toward its northern neighbor. These hurdles include high transportation costs, lack of infrastructure in North Korea (i.e., insufficient and irregular supplies of electricity), the absence of raw materials and other input supplies inside North Korea, complicated government red tape in South Korea, and the lack of legal and institutional frameworks (Yoon, 2000).

Regardless of the eventual outcome and practical implications of such regulatory changes, new legislation over the last couple of years has definitely accelerated North Korea's efforts to attract foreign capital and open its doors to foreign investment. Although U.S. economic sanctions were eased in 1999, North Korea has still failed to attract any significant capital flow, partially due to the Bush administration's hard-line stand against North Korea. In view of the benefits of full North Korean participation in the international community, the Great Powers, particularly the U.S., should work toward building diplomatic and economic ties with North Korea. Such ties will encourage the country to continue developing its open door policy.

CONCLUSION AND RECOMMENDATIONS

During the last half-century, North Korea missed an opportunity for economic prosperity that was achieved by many developing countries around the world, including South Korea. North Korea's economic system, based on the political ideology of *juche* (the principle of self-reliance), may deserve most of the blame. The system ignored globalization and instead sought isolationism. North

III. THE NORTH KOREAN ECONOMY

Korea was over-dependent on the Soviet Union instead of finding new markets, and had not fully utilized its abundant natural resources. The country arrived at a crossroads of whether to maintain the status quo or to reform the existing system. Reform was the better option, and North Korea has moved toward adopting a capitalistic market system and ultimately joining the international community in a growing global market.

The new leadership of Kim Jong Il, North Korea's defense chairman since 1994, gives reason for hope. Several positive reforms have taken place, such as new laws and regulations to increase business cooperation, price and wage adjustments, willingness to work with foreign nations, and improved cooperation with South Korea. Kim Jong Il's multiple visits to Beijing and Moscow for economic observations are helping dispel his profile as an ominous rogue tyrant in Asia, and are reinforcing his transformed image of a decisive, practical and serious leader.

North Korea possesses the basic economic elements to improve its position in the global marketplace. The country is attractive to foreign investment and trade for five reasons (Choe and Huff 2001): the stabilized region, an affordable labor force, a potential consumer market, underdeveloped natural resources, and a strategic distribution location that can be connected to European markets by the Trans-China Railway or the Trans-Siberian Railway.

Along with these positive aspects, North Korea has an urgent need to improve its foreign trade and foreign investment in order to propel the country toward globalization. To accomplish this goal, three strategies are evident: adoption of a marketing concept, expansion of economic partners, and renewed emphasis on inter–Korean economic cooperation.

Adoption of a Marketing Concept. It may seem inappropriate to talk about a marketing concept and a business philosophy for a country in which there is not enough food to feed its own people, but it is important for North Korea to recognize that its economic future largely depends on marketing. In principle, marketing is built on the satisfaction of consumers. No country is stable and strong unless the majority of its consumers are satisfied. Proper dissemination of a marketing concept into the minds of North Koreans at all levels of business and government will be a good start to building the country's economy for the long term. Marketing by North Korea is not limited to product marketing, but also includes "location" marketing, such as the Mt. Kumgang tourism project.

The marketing concept does not have to follow a Western approach. The concept should be appropriate for the unique strengths of North Korea. North Korea should avoid marketing mistakes that are common to those who copied Western approaches without modification. A good starting point would be the examination of mistakes suffered by neighboring Chinese markets.

Expansion of Economic Partners. Excessive reliance on the Soviet/Russian market taught North Korea a difficult lesson. Many countries are eager to purchase the inexpensive but high-quality products that North Korea can deliver. North Korea should evaluate many countries to find potential economic partners who are willing to establish a mutually beneficial relationship. This approach will enhance the image of North Korea and consolidate its position in the world.

Emphasis on Inter-Korean Economic Cooperation. In the short history of trade between the two Koreas, both the volume of trade and the products exchanged indicate a dynamic process. The economic benefits of inter–Korean cooperation support continued expansion of trade and investment. These include cost savings in transportation, the complementary nature of the two separated economies, and, more than anything else, the desire of the people on both sides to work toward the ultimate common goal, Korean unification.

Summary. By increasing inter–Korean commercial contacts—through trade, joint ventures, technology transfer arrangements, infrastructure development projects and other initiatives—it will be possible to diminish tensions in the Korean peninsula as well as to accelerate North Korean internal reform. Proponents of such an approach make four independent but interrelated arguments for their case (Eberstadt, 1999). First, the North Korean system is in desperate need of precisely the advantages that inter–Korean economic cooperation can provide. Second, North

Korean leadership understands the country's economic difficulties and the urgency with which trade opportunities and other international economic contacts must now be pursued. Third, an economic opening in North Korea would be in South Korea's own financial interest, rather than simply an exercise in checkbook diplomacy. Fourth, South Korea has a record of demonstrated success in bringing formerly hostile communist countries to the point of rapprochement through economic diplomacy.

A foundation for expanding inter–Korean economic cooperation has been created since the June 2000 summit meeting. It will be successful if North and South Korea work under the principles of mutual and balanced development. The speed and scope of economic cooperation will depend on such factors as North Korea's attitude toward reform and the opening of its economy, the fundraising ability of the South Korean government and its corporations, and the cooperation and participation of the international community.

KEY TERMS AND CONCEPTS

Inter-Korean trade
Asian financial crisis
Trade imbalance
Trade surplus
Economic sanctions
The Foreign Trade Act

Enforcement Decree of the Foreign Investment Protection Act
Free economic zone
Product marketing
Location marketing

QUESTIONS AND APPLICATION

1. Describe the economic status of North Korea from 1948 to 1975. How is North Korea's economic expansion during this period explained?

2. How did South Korea fare economically from 1948 to 1970? Why was the country lagging behind North Korea?

3. What was the reason for the South Korean economic turn-around in the 1970s?

4. Compare North and South Korean economic standings from 1970s to the end of the 1990s.

5. What is the sunshine policy? How has the sunshine policy affected inter–Korean relations?

6. Aside from increased trade between the North and the South, how would improved inter–Korean relations and cooperation affect South Korea's economy?

7. How would North Korea benefit from numerous smaller trade partners as opposed to a few bigger trade partners?

8. How can North Korea further improve its efforts for globalizations? Which three recommendations have been given in this chapter?

REFERENCES

Choe, Sang T., and Kelly D. Huff. "Five Reasons to Do Business with North Korea." *International Journal of Commerce and Management*, Vol. 12, No. 2, 2002, pp. 31–43.

French, Howard W. "North Korea Adding a Pinch of Capitalism to Its Economy." *New York Times*, August 9, 2002, p. A1.

Kim Dae Jung. "Reconcile, Cooperate, and Live in Peaceful Coexistence." *Presidents and Prime Ministers*, November/December 2000, pp. 22–24.

Korea Herald. "Inter-Korean Trade Up 7.9% This Year." July 26, 2002, p. 5.

Kwon, Daeyol. "Birth of Dollar Store in Pyung Yang." www.chosun.com, July 23, 2002.

Lee, Eric. "Development of North Korea's Legal Regime Governing Foreign Business Cooperation: A Revisit under the New Socialist Constitution of 1998." *Northwestern Journal of International Law & Business*, Fall 2000, pp. 199–242.

III. THE NORTH KOREAN ECONOMY

Lee, Soo-Jeong. "South Korean Report: North Korean Economy Grew 3.7% in 2001." *AP Worldstream*, May 14, 2002.

Noland, Marcus. "The North Korean Economy." *Economic and Regional Cooperation in Northeast Asia, Joint U.S.–Korea Academic Studies*. Vol. 6. Washington, D.C.: Korean Economic Institute of America, 1996, pp. 148–149.

_____, Sherman Robinson, and Tao Wang. "Famine in North Korea: Causes and Cures." *Economic Development and Cultural Change*, July 2001, pp. 741–767.

Park, Dong Whan, ed. *The U.S. and the Two Koreas*. Boulder: Lynne Rienner Publishers, 1988.

Savada, Andrea M. *North Korea: A Country Study*. Washington, D.C.: Library of Congress, 1993, p. 106.

Yoon, Deok-Ryong. "Interaction and Direction of Investment Market between South and North Koreas: Gradual Integration Approach." *Korean Unification Studies*, vol. 7, no. 2, 2000, pp. 86–94.

7 Doing Business with North Korea

SUMMARY

Loss of allies in the early 1990s, consecutive floods in 1995 and 1996, and a severe drought in 1997 shrunk the North Korean economy. While North Korea had gradually reformed its troubled economic system in the 1990s, these measures were limited and different from market-oriented reform. Inter-Korean relations have improved significantly since the historical encounter of two Korean leaders on June 13, 2000. In July 2002, North Korea introduced the most significant liberalization measures since the start of communist rule in 1948 (French, 2002). The conventional explanation for this sudden reversal of North Korean economic policy is that it is desperate for external economic assistance and investment. Such an open-door policy creates opportunities and challenges for foreign governments, companies, and individuals. This chapter discusses reasons to do business with North Korea, entry modes to the North Korean markets, differences in management style between Western and Asian corporations, practical tips on doing business in North Korea, and political risk analysis.

115

Reasons for Doing Business with North Korea

North Korea has worked very hard in recent years to improve the business climate for foreign companies and individual investors in an effort to boost its sagging economy. Although the improved business climate is not a sufficient reason alone for doing business, it is a necessary ingredient for business relations. No external investors or traders will do business with North Korea, or any country for that matter, unless reasonable opportunities for making money exist. Evidence indicates that Pyongyang will continue to improve its business climate so that foreign companies and investors can make money in this impoverished country. If the business climate in North Korea continues to improve as expected, a number of good reasons for doing business with the country surface. North Korea offers the prospect of a regional stability with South Korea, abundant natural resources, a cheap labor force, a market of 22 million people for a wide variety of consumer goods, and a strategic distribution location for Eurasian markets (Choe and Huff, 2001).

Improved Inter-Korean Relations. In early 1998, South Korea's president, Kim Dae Jung, adopted a sunshine policy of engagement with North Korea, a dramatic departure from the previous policy of confrontation. The purpose of this policy was to legally allow individuals, organizations, and even the government to build economic ties with North Korea in spite of Pyongyang's hostility toward the government in Seoul. In other words, the sunshine policy separated humanitarian and business issues from political ones. The leaders of the two Koreas met in Pyongyang on June 13, 2002, for the first time since Korea's division in 1945. Many positive changes have taken place in inter–Korean relations since then; among them, improved regional stability which is sure to result in additional foreign investment and may eventually contribute to even better regional stability and peace.

Underdeveloped Natural Resources. Unlike South Korea, North Korea is rich in natural resources. Pyongyang has at least 40 different natural resources that can be highly valuable in export markets. For example, North Korea is the world's second largest producer of magnesia and earns a substantial amount of hard currencies from its exports. In August 1999, Aurora Partners became the first U.S. Company to form a joint venture with North Korea in order to mine, process, and export magnesia products. Several companies from Israel and Australia have negotiated with North Korea about potential investments in natural resources, but only a small number of foreign investors have actually invested in North Korea so far. North Korea's ability to extract many of its natural resources is limited mainly due to its underdeveloped infrastructure. Its inability to harvest natural resources creates additional opportunities for foreign companies. Thus, the country's natural resources should prove to be one of its primary means of economic development.

Abundant and Affordable Labor Force. North Korea has a labor force of 10 million people, which grows idle as its economy stagnates. In other words, many are unemployed or underemployed mainly due to the lack of capital and technology. Its regime recognizes numerous potential benefits of expanded economic cooperation with South Korea and other countries. To maximize foreign investors' use of abundant labor force, North Korea has recently introduced a host of new laws addressing foreign investment, relations with capital firms, new zones of free trade, and double taxation. If foreign manufacturing operations play a negligible strategic role, tangible benefits, such as reductions in labor, capital, and logistical costs, usually dominate a company's decision to manufacture abroad (Ferdows, 1999). Because no one can expect to realize intangible benefits (i.e., new ideas) from its investment in North Korea, the country is a good place for foreign companies that wish to seek tangible benefits.

Foreign countries and companies could emulate the U.S.-Mexican relationship of *maquiladoras* (export assembly plant) in North Korea. *Maquiladoras* are responsible for approximately one million jobs in Mexico, and they are the source of half of Mexico's exports (Sowinski, 2000). Such a program, called "processing-on-commission," has been thriving between the two Koreas for years. This program involves the transfer of equipment and materials from South Korea to North Korea where the lower labor cost is used to produce goods, which in turn are exported out of North Korea.

Growing Market Potential. North Korea is one of the few remaining countries still untapped by multinational companies and their per capita income is very low. As North Korea's government and labor force begin to receive compensation from its foreign business cooperation and open-door policy, their overall ability and willingness to purchase domestic and foreign goods will undoubtedly increase. In the winter 2002 North Korea announced that it would cut the number of its troops significantly, which is likely to reduce a substantial amount of its military expenditure. The amount of money to be released from decreased military spending would surely increase the purchasing power of 22 million consumers for foreign goods and services.

Coca-Cola was the first U.S. company to export its goods to North Korea after President Clinton lifted some trade sanctions in September 1999. Initially Coca-Cola plans to sell its products in hotels, but the important point is the early jump at market development for future years as Pyongyang's economy improves. Early entrance into the North Korean market may be critical because evidence indicates that foreign trade with developing countries grows at a faster rate than with industrialized countries. North Korea prefers foreign investments in infrastructure areas such as telecommunications, utilities, and transportation.

Strategic Distribution Location. Currently, South Korea must ship and receive goods in foreign trade via air or sea because the division of Korea has prevented South Koreans from shipping or receiving goods via land routes since 1945. Exports and imports among Eurasian markets through the air or sea are lengthy and expensive. Recently, the two Koreas agreed to re-link the severed South-North railway and build a new highway to link the South to Kaesong City just north of the demilitarized zone. This connection should reduce by 15 days the shipment times from South Korea to Europe. Transportation costs between the two Koreas would fall from the current rate of $1,000 per ton to $250 per ton (McMullan, 2000). Observers also predict that by 2025 these lines of transportation will be the cores of economic activities carried by 2.5 billion people producing one-quarter of the world's economy (*Korean Business Review*, 2000).

HOW TO ENTER FOREIGN MARKETS

A company seeking to expand its business into North Korea or any other foreign market will find several distinct alternatives for its business model: exports, new plants, mergers and acquisitions, joint ventures, equity alliances, licensing agreement, franchising agreement, and contract manufacturing.

Exports. Exports are a relatively conservative approach for penetrating foreign markets. There is minimal risk to this approach because a company does not place any of its capital at risk. If the company experiences a decline in exports, it can usually reduce or discontinue this part of its business at a low cost. Many large U.S. companies, such as Boeing, General Electric, and IBM, generate more than $4 billion annually from exports. When a company expands its operations beyond national boundaries for the first time, it tends to exploit foreign markets through exports. However, to become part of a global market, a company must have a worldwide presence. An export-oriented strategy serves a company well initially, but a worldwide presence cannot be sustained by exports alone.

Construction of New Plants (Internal Growth). Companies can penetrate international markets by establishing new operations in foreign countries to produce and sell products. Some companies may prefer such internal growth because they can tailor foreign operations to specific needs. For example, General Motors spent several years analyzing the market size for cars in China before the company decided to build two auto assembly plants in that country. Such a demand forecast or market-size projection depends on many factors, such as competition, income, population, economic conditions, and the feasibility of serving nearby foreign markets. However, it takes time for companies to reap substantial rewards from internal growth because they first have to build plants and establish a customer base.

Mergers and Acquisitions (External Growth). Although internal growth is usually a natural and economical option, the process tends to be slow. These days many companies take an accelerated approach: they acquire existing firms in foreign countries rather than build factories that may take years to complete. Some companies purchase a stake in foreign firms to obtain a foothold in foreign operations. In many cases, companies acquire existing firms to obtain instant access to foreign markets and to reduce competition. For example, in December 1998, British Petroleum purchased Amoco of the United States to expand its U.S. market share and to eliminate one of its major U.S. competitors.

Joint Ventures. A joint venture is a venture owned by two or more firms. Sometimes the partners in a joint venture are from several different countries. Many companies penetrate foreign markets by forming a joint venture with companies already competing in those markets. Most joint ventures permit two companies to maximize their respective competitive advantages in a given project. For example, General Mills of the United States and Nestlé of Switzerland formed a joint venture so that the cereals produced by General Mills could be sold through Nestlé's huge global distribution network.

The basic advantage of a joint venture is that it enables companies to generate incremental revenue or cost savings. A joint venture, however, frequently faces many complex problems. Because representatives of both companies sit on the board of directors, it is difficult to forge a consensus, especially when the partners are a foreign company and a host-country firm. Nevertheless, international joint ventures are increasingly common these days. The proliferation of new technology, the expense of staying on the leading edge, the demands of customers, and worldwide competition have required many companies to form a wide range of joint ventures and partnerships.

Equity Alliances. An equity alliance is an alliance in which one company takes an equity position in another company. In some cases, each party takes an ownership in the other. The purpose of the equity ownership is to solidify a collaborative contract so that it is difficult to dissolve, particularly if the ownership is large enough to secure a board membership for the investing company. The airline industry epitomizes the use of equity alliances. IBM maintains more than 500 equity alliances around the world.

Licensing Agreement. A licensing agreement is an agreement where a company (the licensor) allows a foreign company (the licensee) to produce its products in a foreign country in exchange for royalties, fees, and other forms of compensation. Companies can set up their own production facilities abroad or license local firms to manufacture their products in return for royalties. For example, AT&T has a licensing agreement to build and operate part of India's telephone system.

Advantages to a licensor include: (1) a relatively small amount of investment, (2) an opportunity to penetrate foreign markets, (3) minimal political and financial risks, and (4) an easy way to circumvent foreign-market entry restrictions. Benefits to a licensee include: (1) an inexpensive way to obtain new technology, (2) an easy way to diversify into additional product lines, and (3) an opportunity to capitalize on unique positions, such as channels of distribution, financial resources, and marketing expertise.

Like all aspects of good business, successful licensing requires management and planning. Because there is no global clearinghouse for technology, the matching process stretches around the world with a wide variety of intermediaries. The process is further complicated due to politics, international laws, different cultures, and global secrecy. Consequently, a continuous stream of profitable licensing agreements requires hard thinking, good planning, and substantial outlays for research and development.

Franchising Agreement. A franchising agreement is an agreement where a company (franchiser) allows a foreign company (franchisee) to sell products or services under a highly publicized brand name and a well-established set of procedures. Under such an arrangement, the franchiser allows the franchisee not only to sell products or services but also assists on a continuing basis in the operation of the business.

Franchising is most associated with the United States, accounting for about one-third of U.S. retail sales. Some 500 U.S. franchisers have approximately 50,000 outlets worldwide. Fast-food operations, such as McDonald's, Kentucky Fried Chicken, and Dunkin' Donuts, have the most. McDonald's alone has almost 10,000 restaurants in 100 countries. Other types of franchisers are hotels (Hilton), soft drinks (Coca-Cola), clerical services (Kelly Services), and automotive products (Midas).

Contract Manufacturing. Contract manufacturing occurs when a company contracts with a foreign manufacturer to produce products according to its specifications. The contract manufacturer does not market the products it produces. Instead, the company markets the products under its own brand name. For example, Wal-Mart sells a variety of products made by contract manufacturers under its brand name. Thus, the buying public normally does not know that the selling company did not actually produce the product. In addition, some companies subcontract assembly work or the production of parts to independent companies overseas.

WHICH ARE THE BEST ENTRY MODES TO THE NORTH KOREAN MARKETS?

If a foreign company is interested in doing business with North Korea, it should first examine the reasons why to do business in the first place. If there is a reasonable opportunity for the company to make money there, then it should evaluate a variety of entry modes into North Korean markets to determine which ones are the best for the company. The following section recommends three entry modes: wholly owned subsidiary, contract manufacturing, and equity alliances.

Buy or Build Plants (Wholly Owned Subsidiaries). North
Korea has recently established two free economic zones to attract
foreign investment: a Free Economic and Trade Zone (FETZ) in
the Rajin-Sunbong area and a Special Administrative Zone (SAZ)
in the Shinujiu area. The FETZ is located in the northeastern part
of North Korea on the Tuman River where the boundaries of North
Korea, China, and Russia meet. The SAZ is located at the northwestern part of North Korea near the border of China. Foreign
companies may establish wholly owned subsidiaries only in these
two locations, which intersect through land and marine transport
business links to China, Russia, Japan, and other countries. Both
locations have well-established ports, which can handle millions of
tons of shipments.

North Korea welcomes foreign investments because they
induce the transfer of technology and skills, increase national
employment and domestic wages, contribute to tax revenues,
develop import substitute products, and help increase exports. Foreign companies are advised to locate their manufacturing plants in
these two areas, both of which would be capitalist regions that
secure free capitalism and private ownership with their own legislative, judicial, and executive branches without any interference
from the central government. A foreign company can enjoy a number of advantages from establishing a wholly owned subsidiary in
North Korea. First, it can realize a substantial amount of savings
in labor cost because North Korea has an abundant and affordable
labor force. Second, it can control the quality of products manufactured or assembled.

Equality Alliances (Joint Ventures and Partnerships).
Because North Koreans do not have financial resources to form
joint ventures with foreign companies, they prefer those foreign
companies that willingly accept non-financial factors, such as labor,
land, and marketing expertise. Thus, an equity alliance with a South
Korean company may be an ideal entry mode into North Korea for
several reasons. South Koreans know North Korean culture and
business practice, which will help foreign companies minimize cultural and financial risks. Both North and South Koreans speak the
same language, in spite of the five-decade separation. In addition,

companies from Japan, Europe, and North America can offer extra cushions such as additional capital and technology on the top of those to be provided by their South Korean partners.

Contract Manufacturing. In contract manufacturing, a foreign company must arrange with a local manufacturer to produce parts of a product or even a finished product, though marketing the product is still the responsibility of the foreign company. North Korea welcomes contract manufacturing because it has many underemployed workers and does not know how to export products. Contract manufacturing may be a good use of North Korean labor until further trade issues and other laws are developed between participating countries. Cost savings are the major reason for contract manufacturing, and significant cost savings can be achieved for labor-intensive products by sourcing the product in North Korea. The limited skills, quality, and experience of North Korean workers producing exportable products form the major drawbacks to contract manufacturing.

Multiple Entry Modes. Any of the entry modes described here may be effective means of entering North Korean or any other foreign markets. Many companies utilize a combination of entry modes—particularly exports and direct investments—to maximize benefits. Some analysts think that direct investments in Asia by Western automakers would cause their exports there to drop because this mode of entry is used to set up Asian production. However, direct investment is closely linked to export expansion. For example, direct German investment in North Korea can open the way for German exports, both as inputs for North Korean production and as consumer goods to supply North Korean demand. Direct investment also offers German companies a foothold in North Korean markets from which they can further expand sales. Finally, direct investment can allow German companies to maintain a market position that they initially developed through exports. In many cases, investment in distribution and other essential services increases a supplier's ability to export into a market. Trade between firms and their foreign affiliates can be an efficient means for international trade. Over a third of world trade is estimated to be intrafirm.

WHICH MANAGEMENT STYLE SHOULD BE USED IN NORTH KOREA: AMERICAN OR JAPANESE?

Once foreign companies, especially Western companies, invest in North Korea, they must decide whether to use either American or Japanese management style in running a North Korean subsidiary. Table 7.1 indicates that there are two forms of organizations, which are diametrically opposed in every important respect. It should be emphasized that each has operated successfully in its own environment. The American organization represents a bureaucratic organization, a largely contractual, formal mode of dealing with people, an entity capable of withstanding high turnover and great heterogeneity, whereas the Japanese form relies on stability and homogeneity. Although the bureaucratic form may be effective in short-run conditions of Western mobility and heterogeneity, its inherent weaknesses include alienation and lack of training. Thus, some Japanese management practices—decision by consensus, long-term employment, continuous training, and the godfather system—could be models to address certain American organizational problems in managing Asian subsidiaries of Western companies. However, it is important to remember that both management styles do not apply in their original form any more because the trend toward a global economy has removed many differences in management practice around the world.

Although North Korea has been isolated for the last 50 years, it is still part of North Asia, which includes China, Japan, and Korea. These three countries have much in common: Confucian values, the strict seniority system, a strong work ethic, lifetime employment, close business-government cooperation, the use of Chinese characters as part of their language, and close interrelations throughout history. North Korea or any other centrally planned economy cannot achieve sustainable economic growth without market-oriented reform. As North Korea adopts an open-door economic policy for its own survival, its new economic system will be closer to other Asian systems rather than the American system. Thus, it would be preferable for Western companies to use

**Table 7.1: Differences in the
Management Style Between the
United States and Japan**

American Corporations	Japanese Corporations
Short employment	Lifetime employment
Loyalty has limited value	Loyalty to firm is paramount
Usually top heavy	Usually bottom heavy
Rapid promotion and evaluation	Slow promotion and evaluation
Highly specialized careers	Non-specialized careers
Individual values	Collective values
Individual decision-making	Collective decision-making
Business seen as profit-making entity	Business seen as service to society
Formal, explicit control mechanism	Subtle, implicit control mechanism
Segmented concern	Holistic concern

Source: Ouchi and Jeger, "Type Z Organization: Stability in the Midst of Mobility," *Academy of Management,* April 1978, p. 308.

the Japanese management style in running North Korean operations.

PRACTICAL TIPS ON DOING BUSINESS IN NORTH KOREA

The U.S. formally abolished some trade sanctions in September 1999. North and South Korean leaders held a summit in Pyongyang on June 17, 2000, for the first time since the division of Korea in 1945. These and other recent events have gradually improved the business climate in North Korea for foreign companies. A New York attorney, Michael Hay, who had an extensive business-consulting experience in both Koreas, put the 2001 business climate in Pyongyang as follows: "If one is looking to get rich quickly with limited effort, then there are far better places to try than in North Korea. However, for companies which are either big enough to have grandiose plans, equally grandiose coffers and

126

staying power to match, or else are compact in size so as to offer niche project, product, or service with a defined time line, then it is definitely a place worth looking at. More and more people seem to be waking up to that fact" (Hay, 2001, p. 82).

Hay's 2001 assessment of the business climate in North Korea changed since U.S. President Bush labeled North Korea along with Iran and Iraq as an axis of evil on January 29, 2002. However, indications are that the U.S. hard-line stand toward North Korea would not change the improved business climate in North Korea in the long run. For one thing, no country in the world, with a possible exception of the United States, wishes to isolate North Korea again, either economically or diplomatically. The conventional wisdom is that the U.S. and North Korea will eventually resolve their dispute over Pyongyang's nuclear weapons program peacefully because South Korea, China, Japan, and Russia will not go along with the tailored containment policy of North Korea suggested by the U.S. in December 2002.

Once a foreign company decides to do business with North Korea, it must take a number of precautions. First, nobody should underestimate the lingering hostility and suspicion which remain between the two Koreas. Consequently, it is fallacious to assume that the best conduit toward doing business in Pyongyang is automatically one's Seoul based foreign subsidiary. Second, the failure to go through appropriate channels can make one's efforts fruitless or even counterproductive because the division and compartmentalization of roles and information among various bodies in North Korea are clearly defined and quite striking. Finally, when it comes to visiting North Korea in a business capacity, reliance on foreign entities with an established track record of relations with investment-oriented North Korean agencies is critical. The business climate in North Korea is constantly changing in a breathtaking pace. Hence, when choosing one's foreign subsidiary, the key question is not so much how many times you have done business in the country but, when did you do the last business there?

Here are additional useful tips on doing business in North Korea (Hay, 2001, p. 86):

III. THE NORTH KOREAN ECONOMY

1. Discretion is the key; both in your preparations for entry and once you are there, avoid fanfare.

2. Remember that your behavior in North Korea will weigh heavily in any decision as to whether you get back in. This advice may also apply to what you say, do or write publicly after you have left.

3. Expect an excellent command of English among your North Korean counterparts. This applies in both negotiations and document review. Expect draft contracts to be dissected in detail.

4. Your hosts will have gone to great lengths to arrange meetings. Reciprocate these efforts and courtesy by turning up on time and being well prepared. They will be.

5. If you are not going in with a specific business purpose, do not try to suggest otherwise to your hosts. North Korean officials have had years of experience of foreign corporations signing meaningless "agreements" which ultimately led to nothing. "MOU [memorandum of understanding] fatigue" is very much in evidence among North Korean officials, and they do not enjoy the symptoms.

6. Do not confuse South Korean *won* currency with North Korean *won*. The official exchange rate of the North Korean won is 2.13 to the dollar; then again, expect to chop off zeros on price tags in Pyongyang.

7. Do not expect to be able to stay in daily contact with your head office while in North Korea.

8. Bring along a portable printer with your notebook computer, plus appropriate adaptors and plugs.

9. Electrical voltage is 220 volts; blackouts and brownouts are common, so common sense dictates investing in a flashlight.

10. Leave your cellular phone home. Otherwise you will be required to surrender it for the duration of your stay.

11. Expect to be pleasantly surprised by Pyongyang. Close scrutiny will indeed reveal some serious blemishes, but overall, the city is attractive and well laid out. The capital boasts two luxury hotels, the more established Koryo and the newer Yanggakdo, the latter on an islet in the middle of the Taedong River, which cuts through the city.

12. Try not to ruffle feathers; it is far better to start one's visit on a high than on a hiccup.

13. Exercise great discretion with respect to photography; if in doubt, ask, every time.

14. Throw out any comparisons with Vietnam, Thailand, or others before even thinking about doing business with North Korea.

15. Excellent Kaesong ginseng products and domestically produced cosmetics and spirits make good souvenirs. The Koryo Hotel in particular has a well-stocked gift market.

POLITICAL RISK ANALYSIS

The combination of foreign know-how, technology and capital along with North Korean industriousness, various incentive programs, and affordable labor costs promises a long-lasting business marriage. However, it has not happened to any large extent largely because of political risk. Political risk is nothing more than an assessment of economic opportunity against political odds.

Types of Political Risks. Although there are several different types of political risks, they can be divided into two broad categories: actions that restrict the freedom of a foreign country to operate in a host environment and actions that result in the takeover of alien assets. These two types of political risk no longer exist in certain parts of North Korea because the government has designated a few cities as its free economic zones. These zones would be run just like Hong Kong of China. In recent years, North Korea has repeatedly signaled that open-door policy will not backtrack. Furthermore, the trend toward a global economy has removed most of these two political risks around the world: the expropriation of alien assets and operational restrictions (Kennedy, 1993).

Factors Affecting Political Risks. Countrywide political risks depend on three broad groups of variables: political climate, economic climate, and foreign relations (Kim, Kim, and Kim, 2002, p. 471). A political climate may be measured by tendencies toward subversion, rebellion, or political turmoil. Multinational investors should consider such factors as levels of political violence, the existence of extreme tendencies among political parties, and recurring governmental crises. Investment analysts should make an overall assessment of the economic climate to protect foreign investment from political risks. Relevant economic factors include the likelihood of government intervention in the economy, levels of interest and inflation rates, persistent balance-of-payment deficits, levels of foreign debts, and worsening monetary reserves. Finally, multinational investors should determine the extent to which host countries manifest hostility toward other countries. Important factors here are incidence of conflict with their neighbors, evidence of an arms race, and size of defense budget. North Korea currently has all three types of problems, but it is determined to follow the footsteps of China, which has successfully implemented government-guided capitalism since the 1980s.

Obstacles to Foreign Investment. Perhaps the best way for improving a country's investment climate is to remove obstacles that impede foreign investment. Some governments seek to restrict foreign investment in certain industries. However, many obstacles to foreign investments are unavoidable, inadvert, or unintended (Kim and Song, 1987). Bad roads, primitive port facilities, the lack of local capital, or qualified local technicians constitute unavoidable obstacles to investment in many developing countries. In some cases, a government may permit some obstacles to exist, but for reasons other than their effect on private foreign investment. For example, the existence of a dictatorship in Cuba and the social orientation of Syria deter foreign investment. Finally, there are unintended obstacles that the government of a host country is anxious to avoid. These obstacles include a broad range of conditions from excessive red tape to corruption in courts. Today, North Korea faces these obstacles, and it would take many years to remove them. Thus, the country is not the best place for investment by short-term oriented companies that wish to make quick profits and move on.

On the other hand, foreign investors would likely find it in their firms' best interest to take a long-term view when it comes to investment in North Korea. It is one of the few countries still untapped by multinational companies, which could take advantage of incentive programs and emerging market-based capitalism. The shortage of capital and the desire for economic growth have recently compelled North Korea to institute incentive programs for foreign investors. These include tax incentives, tariff exemptions, remittance guarantees, administrative assistance, protection from competitive investments and imports, and protection from nationalization and political risk. North Korea is slowly but gradually embracing market-oriented capitalism. A positive attitude toward foreign investment, liberalization of trade, a relaxation of the tight state control, and privatization—these are all embraced by foreign investors. North Korean leaders understand that these are the measures for making investment possible by putting companies on the block and allowing foreigners into the market.

Long-Term Prospect. Undoubtedly, North Korea is still the most isolated country in the world. However, North Korea's leader, Kim Jong Il, has apparently reconsidered his father's long-standing policy of self-isolation in favor of an open economy increasingly hospitable to foreign investment and trade. He desires improved economic and political relations with the U.S. and other countries. This new policy is the recognition of the cold fact that the North Korean regime faces certain collapse without foreign investment and assistance in its crumbling economy. Thus, the strained relationship between the U.S. and North Korea under the Bush leadership is unlikely to change Pyongyang's open-door policy in the long run. Most observers believe that North Korea will surely continue to open its market slowly but cautiously.

KEY TERMS AND CONCEPTS

Maquiladoras	Licensing agreement
Processing-on-commission	Franchising agreement
Exports	Contract manufacturing
Mergers and acquisitions	Wholly owned subsidiary
Joint venture	Equality alliance
Equity alliance	

131

III. THE NORTH KOREAN ECONOMY

QUESTIONS AND APPLICATION

1. Name some reasons why multinational companies should consider North Korea as a trade partner.

2. What kinds of business opportunities can North Korea offer foreign firms from its natural resources? Why would North Korea allow outsiders to exploit their natural resources?

3. How can North Korea's impoverished labor force be of benefit to an investor?

4. Explain the term "processing-on-commission."

5. How can the restoration project of the South-North railway and the building of a new highway from the South to Kaesong City in the North benefit South Korea?

6. What is the most conservative way of penetrating a foreign market? Why is this business model not used in the long run by most companies?

7. What is the basic advantage of a joint venture? What is a common problem?

8. What is the basic purpose of equity alliances?

9. Name two ways in which a licensing agreement is beneficial to both the licensor and the licensee.

10. Which entry modes are most suitable for the North Korean market?

11. When considering American and Japanese management style, which is better suited for running operations in North Korea and why?

12. From the list of practical tips for doing business in North Korea, name three business tips that you found most surprising and explain how these differ from your conception of North Korea.

13. Which are the two types of political risks named in this chapter? Has North Korea addressed these risks?

14. Of the three factors affecting political risk in North Korea (namely, political climate, economic climate, and foreign relations), which is the most instable?

REFERENCES

Choe, Sang T., and Kelly D. Huff. "Five Reasons to Do Business with North Korea." *International Journal of Commerce and Management,* Vol. 12, No. 2, 2002, pp. 31–43.

French, Howard W. "North Korea Adding a Pinch of Capitalism to Its Economy." *New York Times,* August 9, 2002, p. A1.

Hay, Michael. "Doing Business in North Korea." In *Korea's Economy 2001.* Washington, D.C.: The Korea Economic Institute, 2001, pp. 82–86.

Kennedy, C.R. "Multinational Corporations and Expropriation Risks." *Multinational Business Review,* Spring 1993, pp. 44–55.

Kim, Suk H., Seung H. Kim, and Kenneth A. Kim. *Global Corporate Finance.* Oxford: Blackwell Publishers, 2002.

_____, and Yoon K. Song. "U.S. Private Investment in Korea." *Columbia Journal of World Business,* Winter 1987, pp. 61–66.

McMullan, Beth. "Waiting for the North: The Inter-Korean Railway Project Gets a Boost from Russia." *Korean Herald,* November 6, 2000.

Ouchi, William G., and Alfred M. Jaeger. "Type Z Organization: Stability in the Midst of Mobility." *Academy of Management,* April 1978, pp. 304–374.

"Rail Across DMZ Spans Two Continents." *Korean Business Review,* September 2000.

Sowinski, Laura L. "Maquiladoras." *World Trade,* September 2000, pp. 88–89.

8 The North Korean Famine and Korean NGOs

by Hyung Suk Kim and Thomas T. Park

SUMMARY

In the late 1980s, the North Korean economy spiraled downward as the country's chief allies—the Soviet Union and China—discontinued new loans and demanded repayment of outstanding loans. By the end of the 1980s, North Korea's economic growth rate had slowed to a minimal level. Shortly thereafter, a series of crises engulfed Pyongyang. The collapse of the Soviet Union and the political upheavals in Eastern Europe had a serious impact on the North Korean economy. Consecutive floods in 1995 and 1996 and a record drought in 1997 caused a massive loss of crops and cultivated land, further decimating the already anemic North Korean economy. Analysts estimate that 18 percent of the country's farmland was permanently destroyed because of these disasters. Considering that 30 percent of the North Korean economy is agricultural, it is not difficult to imagine the magnitude of the impact on the lives of North Korea's citizens. Observers believe that about

Hyung Suk Kim is founder of the Korean Foundation for World Aid. Thomas T. Park is an assistant clinical professor at Wayne State University School of Medicine.

10 percent of North Korea's population, or two million people, died from starvation and related suffering in the 1990s.

In 1998, the South Korean government adopted a sunshine policy of engagement toward North Korea. The major purpose of this policy was to separate humanitarian and business issues from political issues. Since that time, non-government organizations (NGOs) in Korea and elsewhere have played an important role in providing North Korea with humanitarian relief. Because the South Korean government and Korean NGOs have a vested interest in feeding hungry North Koreans, the prospects for future humanitarian aid for North Korea are positive. This chapter discusses the current food and health environment in North Korea, South Korean humanitarian assistance, and information about the charitable actives of two NGOs: one in the United States and another in South Korea.

WHY SHOULD SOUTH KOREANS HELP NORTH KOREANS?

Today many NGOs in South Korea support North Koreans through a variety of humanitarian relief programs. Twenty-six of these NGOs are licensed by the government under the Law on Cooperative Exchange between North and South Korea. Although the organizations are different in terms of their political and religious orientations, they have recently formed the Council of Private Organizations to work together for the North Korean people in the name of humanitarianism and brotherly love. These NGOs consist of four broad categories in terms of their function: organizations for public service, organizations for unification movement, organizations for religious activities, and organizations for vocational activities.

The South Korean people hold two contradictory views about

North Korea: (1) that North Korea is part of their nation, sharing the same bloodlines and heritage and (2) that North Korea is an enemy with a continuous hostility toward South Korea. The group espousing the former view argues that South Korea should help North Korea to overcome its current economic problems. The group espousing the latter view, on the other hand, notes that Pyongyang continues to threaten Seoul with weapons of mass destruction, and thus Seoul should treat Pyongyang accordingly. For this reason, South Korean views on unification with North Korea and on assistance to North Korea fluctuate as political environments shift from one angle to another.

Leaders of some NGOs have recently faced considerable criticism about their philanthropic activities from conservative groups in South Korea. Furthermore, North Koreans and South Korean NGOs have frequently argued over such issues as the transparency of distribution and the promotion of religious activities. Nevertheless, most NGOs carry out their humanitarian mission diligently, with the hope that their activities will relieve North Korean hunger and help the two Koreas ease tensions at the 38th parallel.

The Food Situation in North Korea. The North Korean famine of the 1990s is at least as severe as the greatest famine in modern history: the Ethiopian famine of 1984 and 1985, which led to the death of one million people. Sadly, the most vulnerable groups of people—children, pregnant women, and the elderly— always suffer most from food shortages. In September 1995, North Korea appealed for help to the World Food Program (WFP), the food agency of the United Nations, and to donor countries. The combination of food aid from external sources and positive economic growth has dramatically reduced the number of hungry North Koreans in recent years. However, North Korea does not have sufficient production capacity to accommodate domestic consumption and to compensate for capital depreciation. Thus, the recently improved food condition of North Korea is vulnerable and could evaporate at any time.

In June 2002, North Korean authorities increased the amount of daily food distribution from 250 grams per person to 350 grams per person, thanks to a good harvest of vegetables, wheat, and barley. However, this amount is still only half the minimum daily food consumption of 700 grams recommended by the World Health Organization (WHO). In addition, in July 2002, the government discontinued its food rationing in an attempt to bring price levels closer to realistic levels.

In fact, unmet need for food remains significant in North Korea. In a recent phone interview with the Korean Youth Association, John Powell, the WFP's regional director for Asia, said that the number of North Korean food recipients through the WFP had dropped from 6.4 million in 2001 to 3.4 million in 2002. This reduction in food supply from the WFP affected children most severely, as they accounted for 60 percent of the agency's total recipients. Consequently, numerous North Korean children are reportedly dying from food shortages, malnutrition, and related diseases. A variety of reliable sources indicates that approximately 50 percent of North Korean children have suffered from malnutrition in recent years. This malnutrition rate is higher than that of Bangladesh and India, both of which suffer from chronic and severe malnutrition. Additionally, the medical team of the Korean Foundation for World Aid found that the health condition of North Korean children was worse than that of Afghan children.

As North Koreans have continued to experience shortages in housing, clothing, and food, the government has taken new measures: large wage increases for workers and price increases for everything from food and electricity to housing. However, this economic reform has made it more difficult for North Koreans to obtain food and other necessities because prices in consumer goods have risen much faster than wages. A spokesperson for WFP was quoted as saying that the deteriorating economic condition of North Korea has forced hundreds of thousands of people, including children, to quit work and school so that they can roam around the sea and the mountains in search of food sources.

The Health Care Condition of North Korea. A 2002 study released by the Medical Supply for Children found that about a third of North Korean children less than one year of age did not receive six essential vaccines in 2001. Even university hospitals frequently do not have standard vaccines and medicines available for children. Approximately 70 percent of the medicines these hospitals prescribe are traditional Chinese herbs. Sick children cannot receive proper medical treatment because the health care system of North Korea is on the verge of collapse. This dire condition is largely due to consecutive floods in 1995 and 1996, which destroyed 298 hospitals and reduced the production of medicines by 60 percent. A former nurse at a major North Korean hospital reported that while the North Korean regime boasts of free medical service for everyone, only those who bring their own medicines receive proper medical treatment in hospitals. Even more sadly, an increasing number of children are infected with hepatitis and tuberculosis due to a lack of sterile needles. The International Federation of Red Cross reports that only seven percent of North Korean people use hospitals today.

Food shortages exacerbate medical problems. For example, children afflicted with malnutrition suffer from a variety of diseases due to a sharp decrease in immunity. Some observers report that two thirds of North Korean children under five years old have acute respiratory infections. In addition, 20 percent are known to suffer from diarrhea. These and other diseases have caused the infant mortality rate to increase sharply. Pediatricians note that children suffering from chronic malnutrition often develop permanent abnormal conditions throughout their system, ranging from intestinal dysfunction to psychological damage. They develop such conditions as permanently stunted growth, decline in brain function, heart failure, and visual failure.

Aggressive treatment is necessary to prevent permanent disability for these children. For example, children afflicted with malnutrition should receive antibiotics and injections of Ringer's solution to prevent fatal diarrhea and infectious diseases. A recent study by the U.S. Pediatric Society found that Vitamin A could reduce the death rate of children with respiratory diseases by more than 50 percent. With the epidemic of children under the age of five suffering from respiratory diseases, North Korea needs an extensive supply of Vitamin A. Because North Korean doctors are reasonably well trained and knowledgeable, they can perform admirably when provided with appropriate resources.

North Korea has looked to South Korea for some assistance with its health care system. However, even with its efforts as the country's nearest neighbor, South Korea's medical assistance to North Korea is minimal. Seoul's medical assistance to Pyongyang accounted for only 12 percent of the total assistance in 2000 and 14 percent in 2001. As a result, North Korea requires much more aid in medicines and medical supplies from external sources in order to save the lives of its children. The good news is that international organizations and Korean NGOs are taking responsibility for helping North Korea resolve the intractable problems with its health care system.

KOREAN HUMANITARIAN ASSISTANCE: ISSUES AND OPPORTUNITIES

In the past, the North and South Korean governments had vied for each other's economic assistance. This period of give-and-take started in November 1960 when the North announced its plan to help the South reclaim thousands of acres of farmland, build 100,000 residential houses, and rehabilitate power plants. In November 1977, South Korea expressed its willingness to provide food to North Korea. In September 1984, North Korea provided South Korean flood victims with 7,200 tons of rice and $5.7 million worth of clothes. In turn, the South provided the North with 150,000 tons of rice in June 1995. However, such economic aids were designed for donor countries to boast of their economic strength and to promote their ideology rather than to provide genuine humanitarian assistance.

South Korean private assistance for North Korea began in the early 1990s as one way to solve rice surpluses resulting from several years of good harvests during late 1980s. The Korean Christian Association and a daily newspaper began a campaign to collect rice from farmers and other citizens under the name of "The Loving Rice"; they delivered 10,000 tons of rice to North Korea in July

1990. In 1991, Korean American medical doctors and other overseas Koreans helped North Korea to begin the construction of the Third People's Hospital in Pyongyang. Several Korean non-governmental organizations provided the hospital with a variety of financial and material support so that it could open its doors for full service in 1995.

Since 1995, South Koreans and Koreans overseas have formed numerous NGOs to provide humanitarian assistance to North Korea. The turning point for South Korean assistance came in February 1998 when President Kim Dae Jung announced his sunshine policy of reconciliation with North Korea. This policy legally allowed individuals, organizations, and even the government to provide aid to North Korea. Many positive changes have taken place in North-South Korean relations since then. Thus, South Korean aid for North Korea increased from $31 million in 1998 to $114 million in 2000. In the meantime, international humanitarian assistance for North Korea fell from $359 million in 1999 to $107 million in 2000. International aid for North Korea has decreased even further since 2000 as the standoff between the United States and North Korea over nuclear issues worsened their relationship.

South Korean NGOs played an important role in increasing the total South Korean aid for North Korea. North Koreans acknowledge the importance of private aid in terms of sustainability, stability, and the great solidarity of a nation, though their aid is still smaller than the South Korean government aid. For the last few years, the South Korean government and citizens have provided NGOs with a variety of support, such as funds, transportation, information, and encouragement. As a result, NGOs have recently switched their major activities from emergency aid to aid with long-term implications, such as agricultural and health care assistance.

A Case Study of Two NGOs

This section discusses the charitable activities of two NGOs: one in the United States and another in South Korea. In addition, it looks at the humanitarian code of conduct, which has been accepted by many relief agencies.

The Christian Association for Medical Mission. In the early 1980s, a number of Korean American medical doctors in the metropolitan Detroit area joined together to consider ways to help impoverished residents of third world countries. They began their journey by arranging two Chinese medical doctors, who had a combined annual salary of $720 in China, to come to Wayne State University Medical School. They successfully completed their fellowship training at Wayne State during the 1987-1988 academic year. Apparently, one of the doctors subsequently had a chance to talk with North Korean leader Kim Il Sung. The doctor, who was vice president of the Young Men's Communist Party at that time, introduced his Korean American sponsors to the North Korean government.

This introduction led to fortuitous circumstances for Korean American doctors in Michigan. The Chinese doctor helped several of them (Korean American doctors) to visit North Korea in 1989. The purpose of their trip was to assess the North Korean health care delivery system and to determine what types of medical assistance were most needed. They found that the North Korean health care system was almost non-existent by western standards. North Korea needed to completely restructure and modernize its medical facilities and procedures. These Korean American medical doctors were somewhat surprised when North Korean authorities told them that North Korea would be happy to accept their medical assistance. North Korea even allowed visiting Korean American doctors to hold a restricted worship service with patients in one hospital. It is important to remember that North Korea, a communist state, is officially atheist.

Consequently, several of the Korean American medical doctors, in partnership with Korean American business executives, founded the Christian Association for Medical Mission (CAMM) in 1989 to provide Third World countries with food, clothing, medical supplies and other necessities. For 14 years, CAMM has donated a wide variety of humanitarian aid to North Korea, China, Uganda, Kenya, Nepal, Brazil, Uzbekistan, Thailand, Kenya, Tanzania, Pakistan and Mongolia.

8. The Famine and North Korean NGOs

CAMM has received a lot of attention and publicity for its philanthropic activities from Korean American physicians, businesspeople, and American friends. This publicity has enabled CAMM to establish local CAMM chapters in Atlanta, Boston, Buffalo, Chicago, Dallas, New York, Minneapolis and Seattle. In 1991, CAMM accepted a North Korean offer to adopt a brand new hospital in Pyongyang, called the Third People's Hospital. CAMM's goal was to provide the hospital with modern medical equipment, supplies and technology so that it would be a showcase hospital in adapting some of the strengths of Western health care in North Korea.

The Third People's Hospital, a 500-bed facility, has since become one of the best hospitals in North Korea. CAMM members have visited the hospital at least two times each year with medicine, medical equipment and other medical supplies. Items donated to the hospital by CAMM include 500 beds, several thousand blankets, dental and operating room equipment, an ambulance and much more. CAMM has frequently been compelled to use 40-foot containers to handle heavy equipment and a large volume of items. In June 1995, the North Korean government invited visiting CAMM members to hold a formal opening ceremony for the hospital, and allowed them to hold a Christian worship service in the hospital chapel.

Unfortunately, consecutive natural disasters from 1995 to 1997 caused North Korea to face severe shortages of food, clothing, and clean water. Consequently, CAMM temporarily shifted its charitable activities from a focus on assisting the Third People's Hospital to broad humanitarian aid for the North Korean people. It shipped $40,000 worth of vitamins, $150,000 worth of pharmaceutical supplies, $50,000 worth of blankets and sheets, and 10,000 doses of hepatitis vaccines. In 1997, CAMM helped the hospital open a new library with medical textbooks, journals and reference books donated by its members.

May 1999 was a turning point in strengthening CAMM's cooperative relationship with the North Korean medical community. The North Korean government allowed CAMM to hold a joint medical conference in Pyongyang with participants from the U.S.,

North Korea, and several other countries. This medical sympo-
sium has become an annual event; CAMM members and North
Korean medical doctors held the fifth successful conference in May
2003. It has also continued to ship a variety of medical equipment
and supplies to North Korea several times each year. CAMM
officers estimate that CAMM has donated $6 million worth of med-
ical equipment, supplies, books, and necessities to North Korea
since 1988. Financial and material support from sister organizations such as Korean Food for the Hungry International, World
Medical Relief, Inc. and the Korean Foundation for World Aid
have made it possible for CAMM to ship equipment and supplies
to North Korea.

Today CAMM consists of twelve local chapters with 200
active members. The CAMM board of directors and officers hold
monthly meetings to go over past activities and to plan for the
future. CAMM currently plans to expand its activities by recruit-
ing non–Korean American medical doctors as members, and by
engaging in broad humanitarian relief programs. In the near future,
it wishes to invite North Korean medical doctors to the United
States so they can learn modern medical technology to help the
North Korean people. Those who would like to know more about
CAMM's activities are encouraged to visit *www.camm.net*.

The Korean Foundation for World Aid. The Korean Foundation for World Aid (KFWA) is an international organization
founded in South Korea, dedicated to providing and promoting
health care and humanitarian services in North Korea and other
nations. The founder of KFWA is Dr. Hyung Suk Kim. The extensive efforts of this man have been crucial to the success of the Foundation. Therefore, understanding Dr. Kim's background is essential
to understanding the KFWA.

Even a brief examination of Dr. Kim's story reveals one very
clear reality: A strong vision, combined with unyielding determination, focus, and regard for others is a formula for almost certain
success. This vision—the power of a dream—becomes a defining
and motivating force.

Dr. Kim's father was seriously wounded during the Korean
War and spent an extended period in a veteran's hospital. His

mother was forced to give up her teaching job to live in the hospital and take care of her husband. The future founder of KFWA was born in the hospital during that time. Although Dr. Kim's father was discharged from the hospital after several months, his pain lingered for years. Originally, army doctors had misdiagnosed his illness as chronic tuberculosis. With this misdiagnosis, a variety of medicines and treatments aggravated his health problems. Several years later, doctors found that the senior Kim's pain was caused by the splinters of a shell attached to his lungs. Doctors recommended an operation to remove these splinters, but Mr. Kim's worsening health caused him to decline the operation.

As a result of the continual mishandling of his wounds and subsequent illness, Mr. Kim developed a strong antipathy toward the communist North Koreans. At the same time, he hoped that his only son, Hyung Suk, would grow up to pursue a successful career. In a strange twist, Dr. Kim did not adopt his father's hatred for the North. Instead, Dr. Kim observed with dismay that a divided country could adversely and bitterly affect people's lives. Consequently, in 1995 he quit his promising college teaching job to establish KFWA in order to dedicate himself to providing humanitarian services to North Korea. Initially the senior Kim was devastated by his son's decision, but Mr. Kim eventually became the strongest supporter of KFWA.

Still, the process of founding and directing KFWA has not always been easy for Dr. Kim. In the early days, he spent much time questioning his vision, thinking, "Why should I give up the career my father is proud of and help the North Koreans my father hates so much?" The answer was found in Dr. Kim's philosophy of history and action. Dr. Kim believes there are two types of history scholars: (1) those who only pursue academic achievements and (2) those who use their scholarly understanding to act as agents of change for a better society. When Dr. Kim became a history professor in 1991, he found that he was not satisfied with his teaching job. He agonized over which road he should take: becoming a successful and comfortable professor or becoming an activist for starving North Koreans. By the early 1990s, observers noted that a growing number of North Koreans were dying from starvation and related diseases. Many fled to China in search of better conditions. This news was a catalyst for Dr. Kim's decision to set aside his career as a professor and undertake a humanitarian mission.

It has been almost ten years now, but the memories of the first difficult year are still vivid. When Dr. Kim started KFWA, he had little money, a few supporters, and no full-time staff. Today KFWA has 15 full-time staff members, an annual operating budget of $100,000, and a dynamic board of directors. It is supported by several government agencies in addition to 3,000 institutions and 700,000 individuals. Through persistence and dedication, Dr. Kim has made KFWA the largest non-governmental organization (NGO) among about 30 NGOs in South Korea that engage in charitable activities focused in North Korea. Above all, KFWA donates approximately $10 million worth of medical equipment, supplies, and necessities to North Korea and several other countries every year.

Several ministries of the South Korean government have recognized KFWA as an important NGO through official actions. On February 3, 1997, the Ministry of Foreign Affairs and Trade permitted KFWA to register as a legal foundation. On April 8, 1998, the Ministry of Unification approved KFWA as the sole NGO for North–South Korean cooperation in the area of health care services. In September 1999, the Ministry of Finance and Trade granted KFWA status to receive financial and additional support from the government. In addition, in December 2002, the Ministry of Unification approved KFWA as an agent to arrange family exchange reunions among families that had been divided since the partition of Korea in 1953.

Today, KFWA retains the vision and passion of Dr. Kim's humanitarian principles. KFWA has arranged numerous trips for about 500 South Koreans to visit North Korea for fact-finding missions to help them better understand the humanitarian needs of their fellow citizens in the North. Its major activities are to: (1) modernize children's hospitals, (2) establish children's heart disease centers; (3) feed hungry children; (4) provide children's hospitals with medical equipment and supplies; and (5) provide poor North Koreans with necessities. In addition, KFWA has recently expanded its medical relief programs to include other countries, such as Russia, Uzbekistan, and Afghanistan. In the near future, the United Nations expects to recognize KFWA as an international NGO. KFWA also plans to pursue cooperation and affiliation with international NGOs. Those who would like to know more about KFWA's activities are encouraged to visit *www.kwfw.or.kr.*

The Humanitarian Code of Conduct. Humanitarian relief agencies have faced many challenges in their efforts to help hungry people around the world, because food aid has been politically abused at times. Unpleasant experiences in Bosnia, Somalia and Sudan led in 1993 to the drafting of a set of standards called the Humanitarian Code of Conduct, which was designed to preclude, or at least limit, such abuses. The code, which has been widely accepted by relief agencies, is based on the following principles:

1. The humanitarian imperative is preeminent.

2. Relief aid is calculated, targeted and delivered based on need alone, regardless of race, creed or nationality.

3. Aid will be independent of the foreign policies of both donor and recipient nation.

4. Local culture and customs will be respected.

5. The relief response will cooperate with local institutions and involve joint planning and joint coordination.

6. Aid beneficiaries will be involved in the design and management of the relief program.

7. Relief aid should be programmed to reduce the vulnerability of a society to famines in the future and meet basic needs.

8. Aid will not advance or support political or religious viewpoints.

9. Agencies will be accountable to recipients and donors alike.

10. Agency information to the media will treat disaster victims as dignified human beings, not as objects of pity.

Conclusion

Humanitarian relief programs by South Koreans have significantly alleviated North Korean shortages of food, medicine, and other necessities. However, these programs had a number of drawbacks that should be corrected in the future. For example, the amount of and timing of South Korean aid tended to depend upon political considerations rather than North Korean needs. Moreover, the items of private donations have changed from necessities such as corn and flour to farm surpluses such as apples and oranges. Such shortcomings are highly undesirable in helping North Koreans overcome their food shortages.

The unilateral policy of the South Korean government in assisting North Korea invited criticism because it ignored public participation and international cooperation. In addition, North Korea mistakenly assumed that the massive economic aid from Seoul would continue because of the June 2002 summit. At least for a while, this misunderstanding led North Korea to believe that it really did not need the humanitarian aid from international NGOs, thereby causing such aid to fall significantly. To correct these problems, the South Korean government needs to provide North Korea with at least part of its aid through private organizations in Korea and abroad.

Because North Korean authorities have never experienced a market economy, they do not understand the basic concept of capitalism: the commonly accepted objective of a company is to maximize its profits. As a result, they sometimes believe that it is wrong for South Korean executives to exploit North Korean problems for their profits. Because of this misunderstanding, North Korean authorities have demanded that Korean executives in South Korea and Japan support North Korean programs unrelated to profit making activities. For example, Hyundai Group Chairman Jung Ju Young was once asked by North Korean authorities to build a gymnasium that provided no benefit to the company. In addition, Korean NGOs frequently engage in economic activities beyond pure humanitarian aid, such as contract manufacturing and guarantee of sales for products produced by North Koreans. Thus, North Koreans need to be educated about the difference of business activities and humanitarian aid. At the same time, NGOs should focus on their basic mission, namely humanitarian aid, rather than economic activities. Otherwise, business firms and NGOs might face serious problems in carrying out their activities in North Korea.

KEY TERMS AND CONCEPTS

Non-government organizations
  (NGOs)
World Food Program
Medical Supply for Children
International Federation of Red
  Cross
U.S. Pediatric Society

Korean Christian Association
Third People's Hospital
Christian Association for Med-
  ical Mission
Korean Foundation for World
  Aid
Humanitarian Code of Conduct

QUESTIONS AND APPLICATION

1. What are two contradictory views held by the South Korean people about North Korea?

2. Why has the recent reduction in food supply for North Korea from the World Food Program affected children most severely?

3. Explain how and when South Korean private assistance for North Korea began.

4. Who founded the Korean Foundation for World Aid (KFWA)? Why did this person found KFWA? Briefly discuss its major activities.

5. Discuss the Humanitarian Code of Conduct.

6. The website of the Christian Association for Medical Mission (CAMM) is *www.camm.net*. Access this website to answer the following questions. When and how was CAMM established? Who is the current president of CAMM? What are the principal functions of CAMM?

PART IV

The Case for Reconciliation with North Korea

This final part presents eight compelling reasons for a policy of reconciliation with North Korea. More specifically, it argues why the Great Powers, particularly the United States, should build diplomatic and economic ties with North Korea.

9

Eight Compelling Reasons for a Policy of Reconciliation with North Korea

SUMMARY

North Korea and South Korea are technically still in a state of war because they have not signed a peace treaty since hostilities ended in 1953. While the U.S. and its allies see North Korea as a threat, from the other side of the demilitarized zone, the regime in Pyongyang feels endangered (Chinoy, 2002). Facing 37,000 U.S. troops in South Korea, a hostile administration in Washington, an economy that has staggered from one catastrophe into another, and an isolated regime abandoned by its old patrons, Pyongyang feels pushed against a wall. Many analysts believe that North Korea's recent policy directions indicate substantive internal reform and external engagement. South Korea, Japan, China and Russia wish to help North Korea make its way through its difficult times because they dislike an abrupt shift in the status quo. At the same time, a series of unilateral actions by the Bush administration for the last two years has limited North Korea's options. An important adage is appropriate to this situation: "When a mouse is driven into a corner, it will bite a cat." This chapter presents several compelling reasons why the U.S. should build diplomatic and economic ties with North Korea for durable peace and stability in the Korean peninsula and the surrounding region.

INTRODUCTION

North Korea, one of the world's isolated economies, faces desperate economic conditions. Industrial capital stock is nearly beyond repair due to years of underinvestment and spare-part shortages. The nation has faced food shortages since 1991 resulting from weather-related problems and chronic shortages of fertilizer and fuel. Massive international food aid deliveries have allowed the regime to escape catastrophic economic failure resulting in mass starvation, but the population remains vulnerable to prolonged malnutrition and deteriorating living conditions. Large-scale military spending reduces resources needed for expanding investment and creating consumable goods. In the last few years, the regime strongly emphasized expanding foreign trade links, embracing modern technology, attracting foreign investment and undertaking market-oriented reforms.

President Bush has successfully persuaded many Americans to believe that North Korea is part of an "axis of evil," and that the world should treat the country accordingly. However, many others throughout the world are inclined to help North Korea make its way through its difficult times. The international community is aware that the majority of people in East Asia do not support the U.S. hard-line stand against North Korea. Politically isolated and economically moribund, Pyongyang merely uses the threat of rogue nuclear status to win the world's attention and aid. In fact, we can list eight compelling reasons for an economic policy of engagement and reconciliation with North Korea.

FIRST REASON: U.S. ECONOMIC SANCTIONS AGAINST ITS ADVERSARIES HAVE NOT WORKED

The U.S. has imposed a variety of economic sanctions against many countries, such as Afghanistan, Cuba, Iraq, Libya, North Korea, and South Africa for political reasons. The U.S. had hoped that these sanctions would lead the masses to rebel against their leaders or at least compel them to comply fully with the U.S. demand. However, none of these sanctions has achieved its intended purpose. In fact, these sanctions have backfired and tarnished the credibility of the U.S. as a leader of the free world. Instead, the U.S. has created miserable economic conditions for tens of millions of people around the world that it intended to help through its economic sanctions. Thus, it is about time for the U.S. to recognize its failed policy of economic sanctions and to build economic and diplomatic ties with its adversaries for world peace and stability. A case study of the U.S. economic sanctions against North Korea may help clarify why a policy of engagement and reconciliation with North Korea could significantly affect North Korea's social and economic changes.

After the end of the Korean War, the U.S. adopted a general policy of military containment, diplomatic isolation, and economic sanctions against North Korea. Under these economic sanctions, any amount of remittance from the U.S. to North Korea that exceeds $400 is prohibited. Fortunately, humanitarian aid was not subject to this limitation. A more serious problem is the inclusion of North Korea on the U.S. "black list" of countries that support international terrorism. This designation enables the U.S. to prevent North Korea from joining international organizations such as the International Monetary Fund, the World Bank, and the Asian Development Bank. Without normalization of its diplomatic ties with the U.S., North Korea could not normalize its relations with close U.S. allies.

For more than half a century following the Korean War, the nature of the economic linkage between the U.S. and North Korea was totally nonexistent. Three days after the outbreak of the Korean War, the U.S. Congress approved legislation to ban all exports to North Korea. Over the next four decades, the scope and specificity of U.S. legal sanctions against commercial and financial transactions with North Korea steadily expanded. By the early 1990s, possibilities for any economic contact between the two countries were proscribed by at least 10 separate laws.

Since the end of the Korea War, the U.S. had consistently applied economic sanctions to North Korea in an attempt to destabilize and manipulate the North Korean regime. However, these sanctions were largely ineffective in stopping the country from developing weapons of mass destruction. Still, a series of events since 1994 transformed the relations between the two Koreas from confrontation to reconciliation. One of the most critical factors in this transformation was an emerging openness in the American attitude toward North Korea. South Korea's Kim Dae Jung's sunshine policy enjoyed an unprecedented honeymoon period with the Clinton administration. While the Geneva Agreed Framework in 1994 defused the potential nuclear crisis in Korea at that time, the Perry process—a process of close consultation with South Korea and Japan recommended by former U.S. Defense Secretary William Perry—was instrumental in supporting and facilitating the sunshine policy. However, the new hard-line direction of the Bush administration deteriorated relations with North Korea.

Previously, relations between the U.S. and North Korea had reached a high point in the final months of the Clinton administration. That trend culminated in a visit to Pyongyang by then Secretary of State Madeleine Albright, the highest-level U.S. official to travel to the North. Her visit came just a few weeks after a top North Korean official visited President Clinton in the White House in October 2000. These and other events transformed relations among the two Koreas and the surrounding powers from confrontation to engagement. Consequently, the four Pacific Powers—China, Japan, Russia and the U.S.—expanded the scope of their cooperation in the military, diplomatic and economic arenas. For its part, South Korea increased the level of its cooperation with these four powers during the same period. North Korea gradually improved its relations with South Korea, Japan, and the U.S. until President Bush took office on January 25, 2001, and made known his intention to revert to a tougher line.

The world again watched the U.S. and North Korea approach the brink of war as their leaders, George W. Bush and Kim Jong Il, played a dangerous game. American sanctions would fail again because North Korea is an unlikely candidate for successful sanctions (VanWagenen, 2002). First, North Korean foreign trade is sustained in large part by its relations with China, Japan, and South Korea. The continued and expanded trade of North Korea with these three countries would thus relieve a great deal of the pressure applied by U.S. sanctions. Second, the status of North Korea as a command economy dilutes the effect of U.S. sanctions. Finally, the two unique principles of North Korea—Confucianism and the concept of self-reliance— function to make the population less dependent on foreign trade. Just as the U.S. won the Cold War without armed conflict with the Soviet Union, solutions to the crisis on the Korean peninsula would be engagement and reconciliation, not further disruption.

Second Reason: The U.S. Should Not Use the Famine as Its Diplomatic Tool

No one knows for sure how many North Koreans died from the food shortages in the 1990s because North Korea as a police state restricts or prohibits access to reporters and relief workers. However, international aid organizations estimate that the number of premature deaths from food shortages and related diseases ranged from 1,000,000 to 3,000,000 in the 1990s (Oh and Hassig, 1999). This may be the most severe famine in the modern history. By comparison, the Ethiopian famine led to the deaths of 1,000,000 people during 1984 and 1985 (Noland, Robinson, and Wang, 2001).

In September 1995, North Korea, in a rare admission of vulnerability, appealed for help to the food agency of the United Nations (the World Food Program) and to donor countries. The most controversial question about the North Korean famine of 1995–1999 is not, "Who or what caused it?" but rather, "Who failed to stop it?" (Natsios, 2001). South Korea, Japan, China and Russia could have done much more to help their impoverished neighbor. American policy-makers initially denied the existence of the North Korean famine and then responded inadequately. For the most part, however, Natsios blamed humanitarian aid officials and agencies that failed to act upon clear evidence of starvation which even the obsessively secretive North Korean regime could not entirely disguise.

Predictably, the North Korean economy began to contract as the collapse of the socialist bloc in 1990 deprived the nation of major markets. Floods in 1995 and 1996, followed by a severe drought in 1997, reduced corn production by 50 percent. The contraction of the North Korean economy, combined with these three natural disasters, contributed significantly to the famine (Natsios, 2001). Certainly, North Korea has long been its own worst enemy. It is a rogue state with one of the largest land armies in the world. It has a dismal history of making threats to annihilate South Korea, of continuing rhetorical attacks against the U.S., and of producing weapons of mass destruction. By 1995 North Korea was, with Cuba, one of two remaining communist countries that steadfastly refused to acknowledge the bankruptcy of the great socialist experiment that had begun with the Russian revolution of 1917.

While enjoying economic benefits from South Korean business firms, the North Korean economy finally turned around in 1999. The Bank of Korea estimates that the North Korean economy grew by 6.2 percent in 1999, 1.3 percent in 2000, 3.7 percent in 2001, and 1.2 percent in 2002, after experiencing nine years of successive negative growth. In particular, North Korean grain output recorded gains, and its import volume expanded rapidly during the last few years. In addition, the average operation ratio of several industrial facilities of North Korea increased from 46 percent in February 1997 to 77 percent in 2001 (Lee, 2002). North Korea, however, still does not have sufficient production capacity to accommodate domestic consumption and to compensate for capital depreciation. Consequently, the recent positive economic growth in North Korea is vulnerable and could evaporate at any time.

In light of North Korea's culpability for its own economic

woes, why should developed countries and humanitarian agencies bear any responsibility for the terrible North Korean famine, and why should they revise their behavior in similar situations in the future? The North Korean famine was greatly exacerbated by the fact that donor countries and humanitarian agencies responded to pressure from a powerful chorus of interest groups and politicians. These groups demanded that no food aid be provided until North Korea agreed to behave more responsibly on the international stage and until the regime could demonstrate that the aid would not be diverted from starving citizens to its military. In view of the famine's catastrophic effects, clearly no nation or agency should have allowed political or strategic considerations to supersede the moral obligation of feeding the hungry.

In recent years, more than 200,000 North Koreans have fled into northeastern China in an effort to save themselves and their families from famine. Now they are trapped there, hunted down by Chinese police, and blocked from traveling to South Korea, which says it would willingly receive them. Though less threatening than nuclear weapons programs, this is a dimension of the Korean crisis Washington cannot afford to ignore. Nevertheless, in November 2002 the U.S. began to use the famine as a weapon in its confrontation with North Korea over nuclear weapons. Washington suspended its monthly fuel deliveries to Pyongyang. In addition, the U.S. stopped for all practical purposes its food aid to North Korea in January 2003. The February 8, 2003, editorial page of *New York Times* stated, "Pressuring the North Korean leaders and military programs is sound policy. However, withholding food is shameful and likely to make the refugee problem still worse" (*New York Times*, 2003).

It is in the interest of the U.S. and South Korea to contribute even more generously in the future. In addition to moral and ethical issues, practical considerations are paramount. Politicizing a famine to advance a diplomatic agenda is reprehensible, and it does a great disservice to the cause of peace in the region. Famines are destructive events with unpredictable, long-term consequences. Even if policy makers are unmoved by the ethical considerations of using mass starvation to force any nation to negotiate, they should be concerned about the profoundly destabilizing effects of famines. As mentioned before, hungry North Korean families have increasingly escaped across the border into China and South Korea; far more could follow if the U.S. continues to use hunger as a diplomatic tool. What will the South Koreans and the Chinese do to handle such an influx of refugees? In addition, if a famine initiates a chain of explosive events, U.S. diplomacy may put the 37,000 American troops in South Korea at risk.

THIRD REASON: A MOUSE DRIVEN INTO A CORNER WILL BITE A CAT

An important implication of U.S. relations with North Korea is the impact of those relations on other nations in the region, such as China, Japan, and South Korea. If North Korea faces political and economic problems beyond its control due to U.S. containment policy, there is a distinct possibility that North Korea could invade South Korea out of desperation. In fact, North Korea has repeatedly stated that it will not capitulate without bringing South Korea into a conflict. Seoul's location just 25 miles south of the demilitarized zone makes it virtually impossible to protect from unprovoked artillery attacks. Even with modern anti-battery guided weapons, the greater Seoul metropolitan area could not escape damage that would wreak havoc in the area where about a third of South Korea's population makes its living.

Even without a direct invasion of the South, an induced collapse of North Korea through policies of containment would certainly bring insurmountable problems to South Korea. To absorb some 22 million people whose living standards are no more than one-eighteenth those of South Korean citizens could cost many billions of dollars. Equally serious would be the political impact of bringing into South Korea's fragile democracy a people who had only known Stalinist politics and the worship of the Great Leader Kim Il Sung. Another serious problem concerns possible social chaos from a massive migration of Northerners into the already overpopulated South.

Former South Korean President Kim's sunshine policy was centered on the concept that North Korea's threats arose from insecurity. Abandoned by its old patrons, economically bankrupt, politically isolated, and starving, North Korea saw the pursuit of nuclear weapons and ballistic missiles as its only path to security and survival. South Korea's policy of engagement was designed to reduce this insecurity and end the proliferation of threats. Various incentives such as economic aid, normalized relations and reduced security tensions were provided to give North Korea a stake in the status quo and persuade North Korean leaders that they could best serve their interests by discontinuing the development of weapons of mass destruction (Cha, 2002).

As an extension of this policy, continued engagement and humanitarian aid achieve the same two goals that the Bush administration seeks through its hard-line policy. Hard-liners have traditionally felt that confrontation and containment would force North Korea to collapse or concede to foreign demands. This thinking has proven dangerously incorrect and has contributed to the further destabilization of relations with North Korea. In contrast, engagement and aid together can hasten the demise of the anachronistic elements of the North Korean regime. While direct aid alone may seem to improve the North Korean situation in the short term, it can also create a dangerous "spiral of expectations" among North Korean citizens. This makes engagement even more essential. Humanitarian aid combined with engagement can help prepare for Korean unification by winning over the hearts and minds of the North Korean people.

Fourth Reason: The U.S. Should Facilitate North Korea's Economic Reform

Under the custodianship of Kim Il Sung and Kim Jong Il, the principle of self-reliance has guided North Korea's economic policy. The economic crisis of the 1990s, however, forced North Korea to adopt a host of new laws addressing foreign investment, relations with capitalist firms, and new zones of free trade. North Korea promulgated many internal banking, labor, investment, and tax laws. The government recognized the numerous potential benefits of expanded economic cooperation with South Korea and other countries. Direct benefits included creation of infrastructure and facilities, employee wages paid by South Korea or foreign companies, sale of raw materials, and development of related industries and neighboring areas. Indirect benefits included attraction of foreign capital, improved national risk ratings and the easing of economic sanctions by the U.S. and its allies.

These laws and other economic reforms undertaken by North Korea indicated that the country was serious about stabilizing its domestic economy and improving its living standards. In promoting economic advancement, foreign trade and external economic cooperation received top priority because North Korea recognizes that economic expansion leads to increased demand for foreign currency. In addition, North Korea has recently intensified its diplomatic ties with many countries around the world. For example, Pyongyang used to have diplomatic ties with about two dozen communist allies before 1990, but now it has diplomatic ties with 120 countries (Choe and Huff, 2002). The flurry of diplomatic moves signals the North's intention to resume dialogue with the U.S., which has been stalled since the end of the Clinton administration.

While North Korea had gradually reformed its troubled economic system since the early 1990s, these measures should not be confused with market-oriented reform. North Korea introduced new measures to reinforce its existing, centrally planned economic system. Of course, a centrally planned economy cannot achieve sustainable economic growth without market-oriented reform. As a result, North Korea has been widely perceived to be in a poverty trap, implying that it cannot emerge from this trap without external assistance.

However, Pyongyang has finally begun to introduce highly significant economic liberalization measures, the most significant ones since the start of communist rule in 1948 (French, 2002). In

9. REASONS FOR RECONCILIATION

June 2002, North Korea quietly discontinued passing out regular rations to its 22 million people, replacing that practice with a system of market prices and higher wages. North Korean citizens use these rations to obtain food and other necessities. In addition, North Korea intends to end subsidies to state-owned enterprises and to allow farmers to own farmlands. Finally, North Korea is ready to eliminate a two-tier system in which a separate type of bank note for foreigners' use only forces them to pay inflated prices.

All this is part of a broader plan to scale back state support, allowing prices and wages to rise and giving workers incentive to work harder. Crucial to the experiment will be the improvement of North Korea's tenuous ties with South Korea and the U.S. in order to boost trade and investment. North Korea's recent economic measures, combined with its equally striking shift in diplomatic overtures to South Korea, Japan, the European Union, and other countries suggest a new willingness to break with past practice.

Why has North Korea adopted this market-oriented reform so suddenly? While it is still in its early stages, some North Korean experts suggest that changes have been inspired by China's market reforms of the 1980s. Others compare the reforms to the steps Vietnam took in the 1990s as it gradually opened its economy. Obviously, North Korea hopes that the transformation of its Marxist economy will allow it to cope with chronic shortages, disease, and starvation.

Regardless of the eventual outcome and practical implications of many regulatory and economic changes, the legislation over the last couple of years and new North Korean initiatives have accelerated North Korea's efforts to attract foreign capital and open its doors to foreign investment. Nevertheless, North Korea does not attract any significant capital flow, partially due to U.S. hard-line policy. In view of the benefits of full North Korean participation in the international community, diplomatic and economic ties between North Korea and the Great Powers, particularly the U.S., would encourage an open door policy and internal reform.

Fifth Reason: North Korean Admission of Its Past Mistakes Indicates Its Willingness to Make a Deal

North Korea has recently issued remarkable confessions about its past bad behaviors. First, it issued a rare statement of regret to South Korea almost immediately after a naval confrontation between North and South Korea on June 29, 2002, which caused 50 casualties. Second, at the first Japanese–North Korean summit on September 16, 2002, North Korean leader Kim Jong Il admitted for the first time that the North's agents had kidnapped 11 Japanese citizens in the 1970s and apologized for those actions. Third, from October 3 to October 5, 2002, North Korea and the U.S. had their first high-level contact in Pyongyang after a nearly two-year hiatus. To the Bush administration's surprise, North Koreans admitted to the visiting James Kelly, Assistant Secretary of State, that his evidence about their secret nuclear weapons program was correct.

What lies behind North Korean leader Kim Jong Il's new urge to confess? All these three and other admissions seem motivated by his desire to try to wipe the slate clean, win international credit for candor, and move on to a new focus on domestic economic development. Kim surely knows that the reforms will succeed only if he can put relations with the U.S., Japan, and South Korea on a new footing. Without technical assistance and foreign investments, unilateral reforms in North Korea are destined to fail. In this context, it is clear that the U.S. could build on North Korea's desire to reform its economy by pursuing a negotiated approach to closing down its programs for weapons of mass destruction. Most North Korean experts agree that an effective solution would be a U.S. promise to normalize relations and cooperate with North Korea's reform efforts if North Korea agrees to undertake a verified and permanent abandonment of the weapons programs (Shirk, 2002).

North Korea has repeatedly asserted that it is ready to resolve U.S. concerns about the threats of its nuclear weapons program, but only if Washington promises not to invade and instead takes conciliatory steps. The North Korean regime believes that a reasonable and realistic solution to the nuclear issue should include a nonaggression treaty between North Korea and the U.S. The North rejected the American position that talks on improving ties should occur only after the North dismantles its nuclear weapons program, adopts verifiable controls on missile production and exports, reduces conventional forces along the 38th parallel, and improves human rights.

Like many U.S. experts, Japan and South Korea also believe that North Korea's confession about its nuclear program is a sign that it wants to resolve the matter through negotiations rather than confrontation. These two countries agree that the U.S. should push North Korea to give up its nuclear program. However, Japan and South Korea have made it clear to U.S. government officials that they will not join any U.S. effort to isolate North Korea by cutting off dialogue until it abandons its nuclear weapons program.

North Korea's recent actions have touched off a new round of dissension among Bush administration hard-liners and moderates. Hawks say that North Korea should be forced to abandon its weapons of mass destruction through economic sanctions and other hard-line actions. Others, led by Secretary of State Colin Powell, argue that the North's new candor provides an opportunity, with allies, to pressure Pyongyang into dropping its bid for nuclear weapons. These officials understand that not all members of the "axis of evil" can be treated the same way. North Korea possesses an army of 1.1 million troops, enough plutonium for several nuclear weapons, stocks of chemical and biological weapons, and thousands of artillery rounds deployed just 30 miles north of South Korea's capital city. Significant U.S. forces are based in South Korea, and regional allies are more vulnerable to counterattack than are those near Iraq.

SIXTH REASON: WASHINGTON NEEDS A CONSISTENT POLICY TOWARD NORTH KOREA

The North Korea–U.S. relationship is the most significant external factor that affects the political and economic conditions of North Korea. The U.S. has 37,000 troops stationed in South Korea and dominates the Korean peninsula in the game of influence. Thus, Washington should have a consistent policy toward Northeast Asia and make it known not only for its allies but also for its foes. However, the U.S. stands toward North Korea have been zigzagged so much for the last two years that even some U.S. government officials have been uncertain about their government's specific position at any given point in time.

Since January 2000, a series of unilateral moves and offers for dialogue by the U.S. government have confused and caused North Korean officials to distrust U.S. motives. Subsequent events, combined with North Korea's growing sense of enforced isolationism and international ostracism by the U.S. have dramatically escalated tensions between the two nations. Shortly after taking office, President Bush put North Korean relations on hold until a policy review was conducted. There was a brief respite in early July 2001 when the new administration's policy, under the influence of Secretary of State Colin Powell, validated a continuation of the U.S.–North Korean dialogue. This posture seemed to suggest that the U.S. would hold unconditional talks with North Korea on a variety of issues, such as its nuclear weapons program. North Korea did not formally respond to the American proposal for a dialogue, a mistake on its part, but expressed through other channels its strong concern that the Bush administration operated under a different and more difficult set of principles than the Clinton administration.

North Korea's view of the Bush administration's tougher line was validated on January 29, 2002, when, in his State of the Union address, President Bush labeled North Korea as a member of the "axis of evil," thus extending his war on terrorism. Furthermore, according to Bush, "North Korea is a regime arming with missiles and weapons of mass destruction, while starving its citizens."

Bush's comments were emblematic of a shift from the Clinton-era policy of engagement with North Korea to a new U.S. policy of containment. This new policy seemed to contradict the open-dialogue policy suggested by the Bush administration seven months earlier, thereby throwing observers worldwide into confusion (Cha, 2002). In addition, the "axis of evil" remark put the Bush administration on a collision course with South Korea, which had engaged in broadening economic and diplomatic relations with North Korea since the June 2000 summit between the two Koreas. South Korea was concerned that Bush's tough talk about the North—even though he maintained he was open to negotiation—would perpetuate North Korea's reluctance to sit down for productive discussions of any kind.

On March 10, 2002, the Bush administration confirmed the existence of "a classified Pentagon review," in which tactical nuclear weapons could be used against some countries, including North Korea, in certain situations. In addition, this nuclear posture review included a plan to build smaller nuclear weapons for use in certain battlefield situations. Although administration officials asserted that this policy review did not reflect a change in U.S. policy about the use of nuclear weapons, the U.S. government admitted that the new review took into account recent changes on the world scene, such as weapons of mass destruction developed by North Korea. Arms-control advocates criticized what they called a major shift in the U.S. nuclear policy.

On September 20, 2002, President Bush announced a first-strike doctrine, under which the U.S. would not hesitate to use a military strike against a country such as Iraq or North Korea. It is important to understand that no sovereign state has been tied to any terrorist attack, though some countries have tried to develop weapons of mass destruction (King, 2002). "For 56 years, the world has avoided nuclear weapons use," said John Isaacs of the Center for Arms Control and Non-Proliferation (*USA Today*, 2002). "The Bush administration is now dangerously lowering the threshold for wreaking nuclear devastation because of its inconsistent policy." In fact, former defense secretary William Perry admitted that North Korea sincerely believed it had no other choice but to develop missiles and nuclear weapons for its own defense. A U.S. policy shift from engagement to containment toward North Korea would further reinforce the North Korean belief that it should develop weapons of mass destruction for its own survival. These episodes and others have added confusion to the crisis rather than clarify the situation for observers worldwide.

Seventh Reason: Dialogue Is the Only Viable Way to Resolve the North's Nuclear Issue Peacefully

North Korea's approach to inter–Korean affairs had been deeply animated by the regime's own interpretation of unification: the two nations could be reunited only on North Korean terms. For its part, South Korea's approach to commerce with the North had also been governed and distorted by political considerations. In early 1998, however, the South Korean government departed from its former approach, as part of a new policy of engagement, to separate business from politics. The South's sunshine policy motivated North Korea to demonstrate a long-term commitment to inter–Korean economic cooperation. In fact, many positive changes took place in North–South Korean relations since 1998. For example, both sides agreed to build a cross-border rail link, a cross-border new highway, and industrial parks. Other attempts, successful and unsuccessful, advanced progress on such issues as divided family exchange reunions, the cancellation of U.S.–South Korean military exercises, economic assistance, drafts of agreements on investment protection, double taxation avoidance, and business dispute arbitration.

Under President Clinton, the U.S. drew up plans to bomb Yongbyon in 1994 over possible North Korean weapons activities. That crisis was defused with an energy deal under which Pyongyang agreed to mothball the facility in return for oil shipments and constructions of less threatening nuclear power plants. However, the agreement collapsed in October 2002 when North Korea acknowl-edged its secret nuclear weapons program in violation of the 1994 agreement. The U.S. suspended fuel shipments. In turn, North Korea, expelled UN inspectors in December, got rid of surveillance cameras, and began to move fuel rods from storage to restart a reactor, which experts believe could produce several nuclear weapons within months.

North Korea offered talks with the U.S. to rectify concerns over its nuclear weapons program. However, the Bush administra-tion rejected these proposals, which were actually similar to North Korea's repeated offers over the last 50 years to give up its nuclear weapons program in exchange for a nonaggression pact with the U.S. In a February 3, 2003, Senate hearing on North Korea, some U.S. senators, including the Foreign Relations Committee Chair-man, Richard Lugar, urged the Bush administration to begin direct talks with North Korea without delay. Others testifying at the Sen-ate hearing said that time was not on the side of the U.S. Ashton Carter, a former Defense Department official who helped set the Clinton administration policy on North Korea, warned against the additional possibility that North Korea might sell or trade pluto-nium (Slavin, 2003):

1. Loose nukes could fall into the hands of "warlords of fac-tions" if the North Korean regime suddenly collapsed.
2. The prospect of war in the peninsula could rise if North Korea has a moderate-size nuclear arsenal instead of only one or two bombs it is believed to possess now.
3. Other developing nations would follow North Korea's example.

A self-educated lawyer from a poor family of peach and chicken farmers, Roh Moo Hyun was elected as South Korean pres-ident on December 19, 2002, thanks largely to his pledge to con-tinue his country's sunshine policy of engagement with North Korea. "Success or failure of a U.S. policy toward North Korea is not too big a deal to the American people, but it is a life-or-death matter for South Koreans" (Hiatt, 2003). "Therefore, the U.S.

should consult fully with South Korea, rather than making a decision unilaterally and then expecting South Korea to follow it blindly." He repeatedly expressed genuine concern that U.S. tough lines against North Korea might plunge the Korean peninsula into a nuclear war. He believed that "dialogue is the only viable way to resolve the North's nuclear issue peacefully" (www. cnn.com/world. January 1, 2003). In the absence of such an initiative, the U.S. is likely to find itself on a collision course with Japan, China, and South Korea, all of which support the North Korean demand for face-to-face talks with Washington.

In January 2003, South Korean newspapers reported that President-elect Roh Moo Hyun would adopt three principles as his government's policy on the North Korean nuclear issue: (1) nuclear proliferation in North Korea would not be tolerated; (2) the North Korean nuclear issue should be solved peacefully through dialogue; (3) South Korea should take the initiative in resolving the issue (Shin, 2003). However, in his inaugural address on February 25, 2003, President Roh announced "peace and prosperity" as a new slogan of his policy and guiding principles regarding North Korea.

Roh's plan for resolving inter–Korean disputes is based on four principles: (1) dialogue, (2) mutual trust and reciprocity, (3) international cooperation under the initiative to be taken by principal actors, and (4) public participation and bipartisan cooperation (Kim, 2003). Critics charge that Roh's new policy slogan and its accompanying principles are so broadly populist that they are meaningless in terms of applicability for resolving inter–Korean problems. However, the great symbolic value of Roh's new policy may help him in unifying the Korean people behind his leadership on inter–Korean issues.

Under the third principle of "initiative," he has proposed that the U.S. concede security guarantees to North Korea in return for North Korean promise to halt its nuclear weapons efforts. In addition, China and Japan staunchly support this South Korean policy of engagement and reconciliation with North Korea. However, the Bush administration says that talks will occur only after North Korea abandons its nuclear weapons program. Thus, the dispute displays a growing divergence between Northeast Asian countries

(Beijing, Tokyo, & Seoul) and Washington in their perceptions of North Korea.

Greater China (China, Hong Kong, & Taiwan), Japan, and South Korea are those countries that the U.S. cannot afford to ignore because they possess more than half the world's total foreign reserves and comprise three of the world's ten largest economies. Of all Asia-related issues, China represents the most daunting challenge for the Bush administration. The tasks include: (1) avoiding a misapplication of American unilateralism in the region; (2) averting American policy disunity over North Korea; and (3) pursuing free trade in ways that will make a difference in Asia without domestic political interference (Shuja, 2002). Thus, it is about time for the U.S. to let principal actors in Northeast Asian region—China, Japan, and South Korea—take an initiative on the North Korean issue and focus instead on its war against terrorism. The U.S. policy of engagement and reconciliation with North Korea will make it possible to diminish tensions on the Korean peninsula as well as accelerate North Korean internal reform.

EIGHTH REASON: NEGATIVE OUTCOMES OF THE BUSH ADMINISTRATION'S UNILATERALISM REQUIRE THE U.S. TO ENGAGE OTHER COUNTRIES ON WORLD AFFAIRS

The collapse of the Soviet Union in 1991 along with the unusually strong performance of both the U.S. economy and its stock market during the 1990s elevated the U.S. to unsurpassed economic, military, and cultural power. However, in the early 2000s, the U.S. faced its sixth wave of decline since the 1950s, a phenomenon largely triggered by its aggressive unilateralism. The first wave occurred in 1957 and 1958 when the Soviet Union launched the Sputnik, the first manned satellite. The second wave came at the end of 1960s when President Nixon began to prepare Americans for a multipolar world because an economic and military decline was inevitable for America. The third wave followed immediately after the OPEC oil embargo in 1973 and the dramatic increase in oil prices. The fourth wave took place in the 1970s because of the Vietnam War, Watergate scandal, continued development of Soviet nuclear forces, and expansion of Soviet power in a half-dozen countries such as Afghanistan. The fifth wave happened in the late 1980s largely due to the U.S. foreign debt as well as financial threats from Japan.

Every single empire and great nation of history has been destroyed or greatly diminished in world influence. Why should we assume that the U.S., today's great nation, could defeat the pattern of history? If we assume for a moment an American decline, the European Union or China seems likely to emerge as a great power, which might end the dominance of the U.S. in the game of influence on world affairs. We can base the current wave of decline on three bodies of evidence: (1) mounting U.S. budget and trade deficits, (2) continuing declines in the U.S. economy and its stock market, and (3) a growing European Union resistance to American unilateral actions.

A massive tax cut of $1.35 trillion and a military buildup larger than during the Cold War shifted the government budget from a record surplus of $387 billion predicted for 2004 a few years earlier to a record deficit of $307 in 2004. The cost of the U.S. war with Iraq could increase the deficit to over $400 billion (Neal, 2003). Observers believe that this huge budget deficit is unsustainable and thus will eventually ruin the U.S. economy.

It is no secret that U.S. economic expansion in the 1990s had been sustained with borrowed money abroad. American companies accrued huge debts, often to buy back company shares. American consumer debt is enormous and continues to grow with no end in sight. In addition, the spending boom has generated record trade deficits that grow at a rate of $30 billion a month. To finance current account deficits, the U.S. has been forced to borrow approximately $1 billion a day, most of which comes from foreign investors. Japanese and other foreign investors continue to fund the U.S. economy even today, but the boom in the U.S. economy and its stock

172

market ended in 2000. In addition, nobody thinks that this kind of inflow can be sustained indefinitely as war and terrorism fears mount, causing a change that may boost the inflation rate and hurt corporate profits, the U.S. dollar, and investment returns (www.cnn.com, February 4, 2003). The financial reversal would also bring the collapse of the U.S. security policy and of its calculated strategy of world pacification.

The U.S. should aim to work with other nations on global problems whenever possible because emerging powers—either singly or in coalition—will increasingly constrain U.S. options regionally and limit its strategic influence (Nye, 2002). When President Bush took office on January 25, 2000, his aids assured allies that America was a team player and would practice "multilateralism." However, Bush opposed a considerable number of multilateral treaties and agreements within six months of taking office. For example, the administration had pulled out of the Kyoto Protocol on global warming, announced its intention to withdraw from the Antiballistic Missile Treaty, stated its opposition to the Comprehensive Test Ban Treaty and the International Criminal Court signed by Clinton, backed away from establishing a body to verify the 1972 Biological Weapons Convention, and watered down a small arms control pact (Kupchan, 2002).

Consequently, Bush encountered hostility from U.S. allies in Europe, Asia, and other parts of the world as the U.S. shifted its foreign policy from multilateralism under the Clinton administration to unilateralism under the Bush administration. The threat of terrorism is merely the most alarming example of why the U.S. must seek constructive relations with nations weak and strong. Critics charge that international crises, such as arms conflicts in Iraq and North Korea, simultaneously are "the natural consequences of Bush's unilateralism, his militaristic new doctrine of preemption, and his insistence on expanding a justified war against al Qaeda to a misconstrued axis of evil" (Diehl, 2002). "Previously secure countries can quickly drift away from the political grasp of the hegemony, as resentments and anxieties about the unipolarity of the world grow" (Harold, 2002). Consequently, just as the Roman version of unipolarity collapsed, the U.S. position of unchallenged dominance on world affairs might end as the U.S. continues to rely on unilateral actions to resolve its conflict with other counties.

The weak performance of both the U.S. economy and its stock market in the last few years, a sinking confidence of American people in their government's ability to govern, and growing anti–Americanism around the world indicate a possible decline of the U.S. power economically and militarily. A decline of American hegemony may play itself out over this decade and the next. In turn, the U.S. could lose interest in playing the role of global protector, as the European Union becomes a new center of global power and renews competition for international dominance. If the U.S. is compelled to give away its global power to a more dangerous environment, the chief threat may come not from the likes of Osama bin Laden, but from the return of traditional geopolitical rivalry (Kupchan, 2002).

Conclusion

North Korea and Iraq have dominated the world's attention in recent years, yet in countries and regions around the globe, strife smolders with sporadic notice. The seeds and harvest of conflicts in Africa, Asia, Europe, and South America include civil war, threat of nuclear deployment, human trafficking, and starvation. Neglecting these conflicts may be as dangerous as any other conflict in the world. States that cannot police their own territories are places that dedicated terrorists could infiltrate and threaten (Oglesby, 2003). If the U.S. resolves its conflict with North Korea through dialogue, it can work with other nations together on many global conflicts, which will make a big difference for world peace and stability.

This chapter presented eight compelling reasons for a policy of engagement and reconciliation with North Korea. Most observers and Northeast Asian people have recently advised the Bush administration to begin direct talks with North Korea immediately (Slavin, 2003). After all, all neighboring countries of North

Korea—China, Japan, Russia, and South Korea—prefer a peaceful solution through dialogue to a forced solution through a confrontation. If the Bush administration wants to sustain its international primacy, it will need to unite an increasingly divided world through multilateral actions. The U.S. cannot afford to alienate Northeast Asian countries over North Korean nuclear issues when there is widespread and rising anti–Americanism in Western Europe over Iraq.

KEY TERMS AND CONCEPTS

Axis of evil

Economic sanction

Black list

International terrorism

Agreed Framework of 1994

Famine

The Perry process

The World Food Program

Negative growth

Rations

Two-tier system

First strike doctrine

Tactical nuclear weapons

Peace and prosperity policy

Unilateralism

OPEC

Multilateralism

European Union

Trade deficit

Al Qaeda

Hegemony

QUESTIONS AND APPLICATION

1. Explain why North Korea is an unlikely candidate for successful economic sanctions.

2. According to Andrew Natsios, who was responsible for failing to stop the great North Korean famine?

3. How can continued engagement and humanitarian aid achieve the same goals as those sought by the Bush administration through its hard-line policy?

4. Why has North Korea recently revealed its non-compliance with the Agreed Framework of 1994 and its advanced nuclear technology?

5. What is a first strike policy? Why is this policy dangerous?

6. What possible consequences would result from a U.S. rejection of a North Korean offer for talks over its nuclear weapons program?

7. What is the slogan of South Korean President Noh's policy toward North Korea? List and discuss this policy's guiding principles.

8. List and discuss six waves of American decline.

9. What are three bodies of evidence for the current American decline?

REFERENCES

Cha, Victor D. "Korea's Place in the Axis." *Foreign Affairs*, May/June 2002, pp. 79–92.

_____. "The Rationale for Enhanced Engagement of North Korea." *Asian Survey*, November/December 1999, pp. 845–866.

Chinoy, Mike. "Inside Out: How North Korea Sees the World." www.cnn.com, October 22, 2002.

Choe, Sang T., and Kelly D. Huff. "Five Reasons to Do Business with North Korea." *International Journal of Commerce and Management*, Vol. 12, No. 2, 2002, pp. 31–43.

"The Desperate Refugees of North Korea." *New York Times*, February 8, 2003, p. A30.

Diehl, Jackson. "The Accidental Imperialist." *Washington Post*, December 30, 2002, p. A17.

Eberstadt, Nicholas. "Disparities in Socioeconomic Development in Divided Korea." *Asian Survey*, November/December 2000, pp. 867–893.

Fox News. "North Korea Security Talk Pulled Off Table." www.foxnews.com, July 2, 2002.

French, Howard W. "North Korea Adding a Pinch of Capitalism to Its Economy." *New York Times*, August 9, 2002, p. A1.

9. Reasons for Reconciliation

Harold, James. "Lessons to Learn from the Decline and Fall of Empire." *Financial Times*, December 30, 2002, p. 15.

Harrison, Selig S. "Time to Leave Korea?" *Foreign Affairs*, March/April, 2001, pp. 62–78.

Harvey, Joe. "N. Korea Hits Back at Bush's Evil Tag." www.CNN.com/WORLD, February 1, 2002.

Hiatt, Fred. "Seoul May Not Know Best." *Washington Post*, January 6, 2003, p. A 15.

Kim, Chang-kyun. "Roh Set to Become 7th President." International Edition.chosun.com, February 25, 2003.

King, John. "Bush Outlines First-strike Doctrine." www.cnn.com, September 20, 2002.

Korea Economic Institute of America, ed. *The Political Economy of Korean Reconciliation and Reform*. Washington, D.C.: KEI, 2001.

Kupchan, Charles. *The End of the American Era: U.S. Foreign Policy and the Geopolitics of the 21 Century*. New York: Alfred A. Knopf, 2002.

Lee, Eric. "Development of North Korea's Legal Regime Governing Foreign Business Cooperation: A Revisit under the New Socialist Constitution of 1998." *Northwestern Journal of International Law & Business*, Fall 2000, pp. 199–242.

Natsios, Andrew S. *The Great North Korean Famine*. Washington, D.C.: The United States Institute of Peace Press, 2001.

Neal, Terry M. "Bush Releases Proposed $2.23 Trillion Budget." washingtonpost.com, February 3, 2003.

Noland, Marcus, Sherman Robinson, and Tao Wang. "Famine in North Korea: Causes and Cures." *Economic Development and Cultural Change*, July 2001, pp. 741–767.

"North Korea Says It Has A-Arms Project." *New York Times*, October 17, 2002, p. A8.

Oglesby, Christy. "Conflicts Rage Across the Globe." www.cnn.com, February 3, 2003.

Oh, Kongdan, and Ralph C. Hassig. *North Korea Through the Looking Glass*. Washington, D.C.: Brookings Institution Press, 2000.

Olson, Edward A. "U.S. Security Policy and the Two Koreas." *World Affairs*, Spring 2000, pp. 150–157.

"Pimco's Gross Warns of Dire Times." www.cnn.com, February 4, 2003.

"Roh: Sanctions Could Backfire." www.cnn.com/world, January 1, 2003.

Shin, Jong-ryok, "Roh's Cherishes U.S. Alliance." *The Chosun Ilbo*, January 13, 2003.

IV. THE CASE FOR RECONCILIATION WITH NORTH KOREA

Slavin, Barbara. "Critics Question Tough Talk on Iran, North Korea." *USA Today*, January 31, 2002, p. 8A.

_____. "U.S. Fears Spread of North Korea Nukes." www.usatoday.com, February 4, 2003.

_____, and Laurence McQuillan. "Axis of Evil Scoffs at Speech." *USA Today*, January 31, 2002, p. 1A.

Shirk, Susan. "A New North Korea?" *Washington Post*, October 22, 2002, p. A27.

Shuja, Sharif M. "North-east Asia and U.S. Policy." *Contemporary Review*, August 2002, pp. 73–86.

Sohn, Suk-joo. "U.S.-NK Talks End without Agreement." www.hankooki.com, October 6, 2002.

USA Today. "Bush Team Defends U.S. Nuke Plans." www.usatoday.com, March 10, 2002.

Wagenen, Paul Van. "U.S. Economic Sanctions—Non Traditional Success against North Korea." *Law and Policy in International Business*, Fall 2000, pp. 239–261.

Appendix A: Chronologies

TIMELINE I: THE TURBULENT HISTORY OF THE KOREAN PENINSULA

2333 B.C.: According to Korean legend, the kingdom of Choson is founded at the site of present day Pyongyang.

A.D. 300s: Three kingdoms emerge on the Korean Peninsula; Buddhism and Confucianism are introduced from China.

688: The kingdom of Shilla defeats the other kingdoms, beginning a thirteen-hundred-year period in which Korea is a unified nation.

935–1392: The Koryo dynasty rules Korea. Buddhism declines in influence.

1200s: Mongolians invade Korea; they are expelled by the mid-fourteenth century.

1392–1910: The Yi dynasty rules Korea. Confucianism replaces Buddhism as the state's official ideology.

1592: Japan attacks Korea and is defeated.

1600s: Christian missionaries enter Korea; in response, Korean rulers begin a policy of excluding all foreigners.

1630s: Manchu armies from China invade Korea and force it to

179

pledge loyalty to China; members of the Yi family continue as kings of Korea while paying tribute to China.

1700s: Korea becomes known as the Hermit Kingdom, maintaining little contact with any country outside of China and Japan.

1876: Japan forces Korea to open some ports for trade.

1880s: Korea signs commercial treaties with Russia, the United States, and some European nations.

1894–1905: Japan's military victories over China and Russia give it greater influence in Korea.

1910–1945: Japan annexes Korea and rules it as a colony.

1945: Japan surrenders to the Allies. Following an American proposal, Japanese forces north of the 38th parallel surrender to the Soviet Union; south of it, they surrender to the Americans.

December 1945: Foreign ministers from the allied powers meet in Moscow and propose a five-year trusteeship for Korea.

September 1947: The United Nations votes to sponsor general elections in Korea to determine its future government.

August 15, 1948: UN-sponsored elections are held in the South, resulting in the election of Syngman Rhee as president of the Republic of Korea (ROK); the Soviet Union and North Korea refuse to participate. The ROK's capital is Seoul.

September 9, 1948: Kim Il Sung, backed by the Soviet Union, establishes the Democratic Peoples Republic of Korea (DPRK) in the North, with Pyongyang as its capital. Both the DPRK and the ROK claim to be the only legitimate government for all of Korea.

1948–1950: Ongoing border clashes disturb the peace at the 38th parallel.

June 1949: The U.S. withdraws its occupying forces in South Korea, leaving behind five hundred military advisers.

October 1949: Mao Zedong completes his communist revolution in China, leading to an American debate over "who lost China" and concerns over the spread of communism in Asia.

January 12, 1950: Secretary of State Dean Acheson states that South Korea is outside America's primary security sphere in Asia.

TIMELINE II: TENSIONS ON THE KOREAN PENINSULA

June 25, 1950: North Korean troops invade South Korea. President Harry S Truman orders U.S. air, naval, and ground forces to help defend South Korea. At America's urging, the United Nations passes a resolution demanding that the Communists retreat to the 38th parallel and later ask member nations to aid South Korea.

June–September 1950: North Korean forces occupy most of South Korea and pin down South Korea and American troops in Pusan.

September–October 1950: Allied troops under General Douglas MacArthur successfully land in Inchon, retake South Korea, including Seoul, and push into North Korea. They capture Pyongyang on October 19 and press on toward the Chinese border.

November 1950–January 1951: China intervenes in the war, sending hundreds of thousands of troops into North Korea. They retake Pyongyang and press south of the 38th parallel, recapturing Seoul.

March 14, 1951: Allied troops rally to retake Seoul.

July 1951–July 1953: Truce talks founder on the issue of prisoner repatriation. Fighting continues on a battle line just north of the 38th parallel.

1953–1956: North Korea collectivizes its farmland.

July 27, 1953: An armistice agreement ends the war with nearly 3 million dead. A 2.5-mile-wide buffer zone, called the demilitarized zone (DMZ), is established along the final battle line just north of the 38th parallel. The DMZ is the most heavily guarded border in the world.

1954: Negotiations in Geneva, Switzerland, fail to draw up a permanent peace treaty or settle the question of unifying Korea.

1956: After having the South Korean constitution amended to permit him to run again, Rhee wins a third term as South Korea's president.

1960: Rhee wins a fourth term as South Korea's president, but widespread student demonstration leads him to resign. Yun Po Sun replaces him as president.

1961: A group of military officers led by General Park Chung Hee overthrows Yun Po Sun's government. North Korea signs military aid agreement with China and the Soviet Union.

1961–1979: Park Chung Hee leads South Korea to an era of "guided capitalism" in which the government concentrates on building industries and promoting exports.

1968: Thirty North Korean commando troops raid Seoul. Frequent clashes erupt around the demilitarized zone. North Korea seizes the U.S. intelligence ship *Pueblo* in the Sea of Japan.

1971: Kim Dae Jung almost defeats Park Chung Hee in a presidential election. North and South Korean representatives begin to hold talks about reunifications.

1972: Park Chung Hee forces through a new constitution that gives him the most unlimited powers and provides for presidential elections to be decided by an electoral college whose members are chosen by Park supporters.

August 15, 1974: A North Korean agent attempts to assassinate Park Hung Hee but kills the first lady instead.

1977: The U.S. announces plans for gradual withdrawal of U.S. troops in South Korea. North Korea announces that Kim Il Sung's son, Kim Jong Il, will become leader upon his father's death or retirement.

1979: Political dissident Kim Young Sam is expelled from parliament. Park Chung Hee is assassinated by his own security chief.

1980: Chun Doo Hwan, a South Korean general, takes over the government and bans political meetings. Kim Young Sam is placed under house arrest. In May, political protests in Kwangju are put down by force; two hundred people are killed, according to official government estimates. Kim Dae Jung is accused of planning the Kwangju demonstrations and is sentenced to death.

1981: President Ronald Reagan announces that no more U.S. troops will be withdrawn from South Korea. He invites Chun Doo Hwan to visit him on the condition that Kim Dae Jung's life is spared.

1983: North Korean agents plant a bomb in Burma killing 17 members of a visiting South Korean delegation, including four Cabinet ministers.

1985: North Korea signs the Nuclear Non-Proliferation Treaty.

1986: U.S. intelligence detects evidence of a nuclear weapons program in North Korea.

1987: A bomb explodes on a Korean Air Lines jet, killing all 115 on board. North Korea is held responsible. Responding to widespread demonstrations, Roh Tae Woo, a general and Chun Doo Hwan's appointed successor as president, declares in June that he will run for president in a free election based on popular vote.

1988: Roh Tae Woo takes 37 percent of the vote after Kim Young Sam and Kim Dae Jung split the opposition vote; Roh's Democratic Justice Party suffers defeat in parliamentary elections. South Korea hosts the Summer Olympics; North Korea refuses to participate. The U.S. begins to convert diplomatic dialogue with North Korea.

1988–1991: The end of the Cold War and the collapse of the Soviet Union deprive North Korea of its most important allies and economic partners.

1990: Roh Tae Woo joins political forces with Kim Young Sam. South Korea establishes diplomatic relations with the Soviet Union.

1991: Talks between representatives of North and South Korea lead to several agreements, including one not to use force on each other.

1992: Kim Young Sam wins the presidential election; he becomes the first South Korean president without a military background since 1960. South Korea establishes diplomatic relations with China.

1993: North Korea withdraws from the international Nuclear Non-Proliferation Treaty.

1994: Kim Il Sung, supreme leader of North Korea since 1948, dies; Kim Jong Il succeeds him. North Korea and the United States complete an "Agreement Framework" in which North Korea promises to freeze its nuclear program in exchange for assistance in building civilian nuclear reactors.

1995: Massive floods in North Korea exacerbate food shortages; the U.S. and other nations provide assistance; North Korea breaks with its *juche* philosophy of self-reliance in accepting; over the next four years, between 1 and 3 million North Koreans die of hunger, according to foreign estimates. Roh Tae Woo and Chun Doo Whan are arrested in South Korea on charges of corruption. They are sentenced to prison upon conviction in 1996.

Spring 1996: North Korea and the U.S. began talks on missile proliferation. The United States imposes sanctions on North Korea for selling missile technology to Iran.

September 1996: A North Korean spy submarine runs aground off South Korea's east coast. Thirteen South Korean soldiers and civilians and 24 North Korean commandos are killed in the massive manhunt that ensues.

1997: A financial crisis in South Korea results in a bailout by the International Monetary Fund.

1998: President Kim Dae Jung of South Korea announces a "Sunshine Policy" of improving relations with North Korea through peace and cooperation. North Korea fires a medium-range ballistic missile over Japan. The U.S., North and South Korea, and China begin four-way talks aimed at replacing the 1953 Armistice Agreement ending the Korean War with a permanent peace treaty; progress is hindered by disagreements over who should sign such a treaty and the presence of U.S. soldiers in South Korea.

September 1999: The U.S. says it will lift some economic sanctions against North Korea, which announces a halt in missile testing one week later.

June 2000: North Korean leader Kim Jong Il and South Korean president Kim Dae Jong meet at a historic summit in Pyongyang; the leaders sign a joint declaration stating that they have "agreed to resolve" the question of reunification. The U.S. relaxes some economic sanctions on North Korea.

August 2000: One hundred people each from North Korea and South Korea travel to the other nations to meet with relatives separated from each other since the Korean War. A second family reunion event is held in December 2000.

September 2000: North and South Korea defense ministry officials engage in official talks for the first time since the Korean War.

October 2000: U.S. secretary of state Madeleine Albright visits North Korea. She receives assurances that no plans exist to test missiles, but the two countries cannot reach an official agreement.

December 2000: South Korean President Kim Dae Jung is presented with the Nobel Peace Prize in recognition of his efforts to establish relations with communist North Korea.

January 2001: Upon taking office, President George W. Bush suspends diplomatic talks with North Korea and orders a review of American policy.

March 2001: South Korean Kim Dae Jung meets with President George W. Bush. North Korea cancels ministerial talks with the South after Bush states the North poses a threat to the region and cannot be trusted to honor agreements.

June 2001: President Bush announces the completion of a North Korean policy review and calls for "serious discussions" on a "broad agenda" with North Korea. The North Korean government refuses to engage in talks, arguing that the U.S. is setting unacceptable preconditions.

October 2001: North Korea postpones plans to hold reunions of families separated since the Korean War, citing a warlike situation in Seoul since the September 11 terrorist attacks in the U.S.

December 2001: A report by the South Korean defense ministry concludes that North Korea possesses enough plutonium to construct one or two nuclear bombs but that it would take several years for North Korea to make such weapons.

January 2002: President Bush accuses North Korea of being part of an "axis of evil" for developing weapons of mass destruction.

February 2002: President Bush visits South Korea and stresses his support for diplomatic efforts to bring North and South Korea closer but expresses opposition to "a regime that tolerates starvation."

March 2002: Twenty-five North Korean asylum seekers storm Spain's embassy in Beijing in an attempt to defect to the South.

April 4, 2002: North Korea says it will resume dialogue with the United States, but warned it will call off any future talks if Washington "slanders" the communist country again. The announcement is made while South Korea's Lim Dong-won is in the country on a peace mission.

April 25, 2002: North Korean Defense Minister Kim II Chol tells the army to deal "merciless blows" if the U.S. or other forces put so much as a toe over the border. He gives the speech at the 70th anniversary celebration of the North Korean people's army.

June 29, 2002: A violent skirmish between North and South Korean navies on the Yellow Sea leaves at least four South Korean sailors dead and at least 19 others injured. An estimated 13 North Korean sailors are killed when the South returns fire.

July 25, 2002: North Korea issues a statement of "regret" for the Yellow Sea naval clash. South Korea accepts the apology.

August 12–14, 2002: The two Koreas hold ministerial talks in Seoul.

September 2002: Hundreds of separated Korean families meet for the first time in emotional reunions.

October 2002: North Korea surprises the world by admitting that the secretive communist state continued a secret nuclear weapons program after agreeing to freeze it in 1994, creating tensions with the international community.

December 2002: Roh Moo Hyun wins South Korea's presidential election. President elect Noh, who champions President Kim Dae Jung's sunshine policy, vows to ease tensions over Pyongyang's nuclear weapons program through dialogue.

January 2003: North Korea announces its withdrawal from the Non-Proliferation Treaty with immediate effect.

February 2003: North Korea threatens it will abandon the 1953 armistice if the United States continues its military buildup in the region.

TIMELINE III: COUNTDOWN TO NUCLEAR CRISIS

Facts About the Nuclear Non-Proliferation Treaty

• Countries that have nuclear weapons will not help other countries obtain or develop them. Non-weapons states agree not to try to get nuclear arms.

• Countries with nuclear weapons will negotiate for nuclear disarmament.

• Countries without nuclear weapons will allow the International Atomic Energy Agency to oversee their nuclear facilities.

• Countries will exchange peaceful nuclear technology.

• The treaty entered into force in 1970, signed by 187 countries. It was extended indefinitely in 1995.

• India, Pakistan, Israel, and Cuba are the only countries that have not signed on.

1950s: The U.S. introduces nuclear weapons to Korea. (Today it seeks to keep the peninsula nuke-free.)

1953: President Eisenhower hints that he would use nuclear weapons if necessary to end the Korean War.

1958: The U.S. places nuclear-tipped rockets in South Korea.

Meanwhile, North Korea receives Soviet help in training and funding its nascent nuclear-research program.

1965: North Korea receives its first nuclear reactor, a 12-megawatt medical and industrial research model from the Soviets and installs it in Yongbyon.

1968: Great Britain, the U.S., and the Soviet Union sign a Treaty on the Non-Proliferation of Nuclear Weapons, usually called the Nuclear Non-Proliferation Treaty (NPT) to halt the spread of atomic weapons.

March 5, 1970: The United Nations (UN) approves the NPT. Under the treaty, five permanent members of the UN Security Council, China, France, Great Britain, the Soviet Union, and the United States agree not to transfer nuclear weapons to other countries. In addition, the UN creates the International Atomic Energy Agency to monitor the treaty.

April 25, 1975: South Korea joins the Nuclear Non-Proliferation Treaty.

1984–1985: A new 5-megawatt reactor is completed in Yongbyon. North Korea signs the Nuclear Non-Proliferation Treaty but later fails to allow monitoring of its facilities.

December 12, 1985: North Korea joins the Nuclear Non-Proliferation Treaty.

1991–1992: President Bush withdraws all tactical nuclear weapons deployed abroad, including those in South Korea. North Korea submits to inspections of its nuclear facilities.

1993: North Korea says it quit the Nuclear Non-Proliferation Treaty amid suspicions that it is developing nuclear weapons. It later reverses that decision.

1994: After Jimmy Carter intervenes, North Korea agrees to freeze its nuclear program in return for fuel oil and help building pro-liferation-resistant reactors.

1998: The U.S. demands that North Korea stop sales of missile technology to rogue states, North Korea asks for compensation, and it fires a multistage missile into the Pacific Ocean, proving it can strike any part of Japan's territory.

May 25–28, 1999: Former Defense Secretary William Perry visits North Korea and delivers a U.S. disarmament proposal.

September 13, 1999: North Korea pledges to freeze long-range missile tests.

September 17, 1999: President Bill Clinton eases economic sanctions against North Korea.

December 1999: A U.S. led consortium signs a $4.6 billion contract for two safer, Western-developed light-water nuclear reactors in North Korea.

July 2000: North Korea again threatens to restart its nuclear program if Washington does not compensate for the loss of electricity caused by delays in building nuclear power plants.

June 2001: North Korea warns it will reconsider its moratorium on missile tests if the Bush administration does not resume contacts aimed at normalizing relations.

July 2001: The U.S. State Department reports North Korea is going ahead with development of its long-range missile. A Bush administration official says North Korea conducts an engine test of the Taepodong-1 missile.

December 2001: President Bush warns Iraq and North Korea that they will be held accountable if they developed weapons of mass destruction that would be used to terrorize nations.

January 29, 2002: Bush labels North Korea, Iran, and Iraq as an axis of evil in his State of the Union address. "By seeking weapons of mass destruction, these regimes pose a grave and growing danger," he says.

October 4, 2002: North Korean officials tell visiting U.S. delegation that the country has a second covert nuclear weapons program in violation of the 1994 agreement—a program using enriched uranium.

October 16, 2002: U.S. officials publicly reveal discovery of North Korea's nuclear weapons program.

October 26, 2002: President Bush, Japanese Prime Minister Koizumi, and South Korean President Kim meet at an Asian-Pacific regional summit in Mexico and agree to seek a peaceful end to the North's nuclear program.

November 11, 2002: The U.S. halts oil supplies to North Korea promised under the 1994 deal.

December 12, 2002: North Korea reactivates nuclear facilities at Yongbyon that were frozen under the 1994 deal with the U.S.

December 13, 2002: North Korea asks the International Atomic Energy Agency (IAEA), the UN nuclear watchdog, to remove monitoring seals and cameras from its nuclear facilities.

December 14, 2002: The International Atomic Energy Agency urges North Korea to retract its decision to reactivate its nuclear facilities and abide by its obligations under the Nuclear Non-Proliferation Treaty.

December 21, 2002: North Korea removes monitoring seals and cameras from its nuclear facilities.

January 10, 2003: North Korea withdraws from the Nuclear Non-Proliferation Treaty.

January 28, 2003: South Korean envoy Lim Dong-won meets North Korea's number two leader Kim Yong Nam. Lim says North Korean leader Kim Jong Il has received the letter from President Kim Dae Jung that suggests Pyongyang should reverse its withdrawal from the Nuclear Non-Proliferation Treaty.

February 3, 2003: The U.S. Defense Secretary Donald Rumsfeld signs a "prepare to deploy" order that will send 24 bombers to the Pacific region.

February 4, 2003: Pyongyang describes the U.S. move as an attempt "to crush us to death."

February 5, 2003: North Korea's official news agency says the nation has reactivated its nuclear power facilities.

February 12, 2003: The 35-member IAEA board of governors declares North Korea in breach of atomic safeguards and refers the case to the UN Security Council.

February 18, 2003: The North Korean People's Army threatens it will abandon the 1953 Korean War armistice if the U.S. continues its military buildup in the region.

February 26, 2003: The United States says North Korea has reactivated its 5-megawatt nuclear reactor at Yongbyon.

March 10, 2003: North Korea test fires another surface-to-vessel anti-ship missile into the Sea of Japan, or East Sea as it is known in South Korea.

March 29, 2003: Pyongyang says it will resist all international demands to allow nuclear inspections.

April 5, 2003: North Korea says it won't recognize any ruling made by the U.N. Security Council.

April 12, 2003: In a dramatic shift, North Korea backtracks on its calls for direct "face-to-face" talks with Washington, saying it will consider any format for dialogue if the United States is prepared to make a "bold switchover."

Appendix B: Think Tanks for Korean Studies

There are 26 institutions in the United States and abroad that focus on Korean policy issues or include Korea as part of their overall research activities. They are listed below. Each entry has a common format: contact information, organizational status, background/scope, areas of research, and geographic focus. I extracted this information from NIRA's World Directory of Think Tanks 1998 and 2002. This information is reprinted with permission from the National Institute for Research Advancement (NIRA).

ASIA PACIFIC POLICY CENTER (APPC)

Three Lafayette Centre, 1155 21st Street, NW, Suite 210, Washington, D.C. 20036, United States
tel:1-202-223-7258 fax:1-202-223-7280
e-mail: *info@apd.po.my* URL:*http://www.apdc.com.my/apdc*

Organizational Status: Independent institute, founded in 1993.

Background/Scope: Established as a non-profit institution, APPC seeks closer ties between business and political leaders in the United States and their counterparts in Asia and the Pacific. The APPC aims at an engaged and creative U.S. role in the region, encompassing commercial, economic, political and security issues. The Center does not engage in lobbying but promotes instead a bipartisan American commitment to the Asia-Pacific area, offering pragmatic, issue-by-issue analysis of U.S.–Asia trends, rather than advocating a particular agenda. The APPC's Washington activities tend toward informal, recurrent consultation and briefing between the government policy community, and corporate or other institutional executives with responsibility for, or interest in, the Asia Pacific region. The Center's objective is to establish a pragmatic, real-world perspective on U.S.–Asia relations among business and political leaders on both sides of the Pacific. The APPC's operational programs generally result from specific requests from the Center's corporate, government or individual supporters. All the resulting product enters the public domain in the form of reports, conference proceedings, and media interviews with APPC staff.

Areas of Research: Economic, regional security, political and cultural issues.

Geographic Focus: All Asian countries and regions.

ASIA/PACIFIC RESEARCH CENTER (A/PARC)

Encina Hall, Room E 301, Stanford University,
Stanford, CA 94305-6055, United States
tel:1-650-723-9741 fax:1-650-723-6530
e-mail:*Asia-Pacific-Research-Center@stanford.edu*
URL:*http://www.stanford.edu/group/APARC*

Organizational Status: University-affiliated institute, founded in 1977.

Background/Scope: A/PARC was founded in order to foster collaborative and interdisciplinary research on contemporary Asia and U.S.–Asian relations among Stanford faculty members and with colleagues outside the university. Much of the Center's work is policy relevant. Over time, the Center's work has shifted from a country focus to a broader regional perspective, and from a principal research interest in security issues to political economy and regional dynamics more broadly defined.

Areas of Research: Political issues, foreign relations and diplomacy, security and defense, economic issues, development studies, regional studies, social issues, health and welfare, science and technology. A/PARC's current projects include: 1) U.S.–Japan and U.S.–Korea Security Alliances, 2) Urban Dynamics of East Asia, 3) Economic Reform and Growth of China, 4) Silicon Valley and High-tech Clusters in East Asia, 5) Healthcare Delivery in Japan and in the U.S., 6) Reform of the Indian Economy.

Geographic Focus: Asia-Pacific region.

ASIA SOCIETY

725 Park Avenue, New York, NY 10021-5088, United States
tel:1-212-288-6400 fax:1-212-517-8315
URL:*http://www.asiasociety.org*

Organizational Status: Independent NGO, founded in 1956.

Background/Scope: From its founding as an educational organization dedicated to fostering communications between Americans and Asians, the Asia Society has provided commentary on political issues that affect Asians and Americans, new and innovative ways to educate those who educate our young people, opportunities to see authentic Asian art and performing artists, and forums for top government and business leaders of both continents to meet for the exchange of ideas. Today the activities of the Asia Society span numerous areas of expertise and take place throughout the United States and on both sides of the Pacific. The Society pub-

195

lishes scholarly commentaries and analyses of issues that affect Asians and Americans. It sponsors international seminars and conferences for business people and journalists on various aspects of Asian affairs, and provides a forum for Asian and American government, academic and corporate leaders to study and address issues of common concern.

Areas of Research: Foreign relations and diplomacy, security and defense, economic issues, political issues, regional studies.

Geographic Focus: All Asian countries and regions.

THE BROOKINGS INSTITUTION

1775 Massachusetts Ave. NW, Washington
D.C. 20036, United States
tel:1-202-797-6000 fax:1-202-797-6004
e-mail:*brookinfo@brook.edu*
URL:*http://www.brook.edu*

Organizational Status: Independent institute, founded in 1916.

Background/Scope: In its research, the Brookings Institution functions as an independent analyst and critic, committed to publishing its findings for the information of the public. In its conferences and activities, it serves as a bridge between scholarship and public policy, bringing new knowledge to the attention of decision-makers and affording scholars a better insight into public policy issues. The Institution traces its beginnings to 1916 with the founding of the Institute for Government Research, the first private organization devoted to public policy issues at the national level. In 1922 and 1924, the Institute was joined by two supporting sister organizations, the Institute of Economics and the Robert Brookings Graduate School. In 1927, these three groups were consolidated into one institution, named in honor of Robert Somers Brookings (1850–1932), a St. Louis businessman whose leadership shaped the earlier organizations. Brookings is financed largely by endowment and by the support of philanthropic foundations, corporations, and private individuals. Its funds are devoted to carrying out its own research and educational activities. It also undertakes some unclassified government contract studies, reserving the right to publish its findings.

Geographic Focus: Domestic, international.

CENTER FOR INTERNATIONAL STUDIES

College of Social Sciences, Seoul National University, San 56-1, Shinrim-dong, Kwanak-gu Seoul, 151-742, Korea
tel:82-2-880-6310/11 fax:82-2-874-4115
e-mail:*cissnu@plaza1.snu.ac.kr*

Organizational Status: University-affiliated institute, founded in 1972.

Background/Scope: The Center for International Studies is the first and principal research institution in the field of international relations at Seoul National University. The Center renders valuable services to the intellectual community of the nation as well as the University, conducting diverse and interdisciplinary research activities in such areas as international political economy, foreign policies, strategic and security issues, arms control, and the problems of national unification.

Areas of Research: Foreign relations and diplomacy, security and defense, regional studies, political issues, culture and religion. Special focus on: peace, arms control, disarmament in the Korean peninsula; Korea's growing ties with former socialist countries; and the emerging political and economic regional order in post–cold war Asia.

Geographic Focus: Global/international, especially Northeast Asia and Asia-Pacific.

CENTER FOR NATIONAL POLICY (CNP)

One Massachusetts Avenue, NW, Suite
333, Washington, D.C. 20001, United States
tel:1-202-682-1800 fax:1-202-682-1818
e-mail:*cnp@access.digex.net*
URL:*http://www.cnponline.org/*

Organizational Status: Independent institute, founded in 1981.

Background/Scope: CNP was formed as a progressive policy organization committed to the ideal of a vital public sector. The CNP program promotes practical opportunities to advance the public policy process, as experts and decision-makers debate significant U.S. national interests both at home and abroad. CNP activities facilitate policy development by: 1) identifying emerging issues of national interest; 2) assessing policy alternatives; 3) exploring public attitudes and opinions; 4) convening people from different perspectives, in public and private forums, to identify areas of common ground; 5) brokering consensus; and 6) promoting attention to better policy approaches.

Areas of Research: Economic issues, political issues, foreign relations and diplomacy, regional studies, labor and human resource development, security and defense, industry policy, development studies, social issues, education, science and technology, environment and natural resources.

Geographic Focus: Domestic with emphasis on foreign policy issues, Cyprus, Korea, Cambodia, Southeast Asia.

CENTER FOR PACIFIC ASIA STUDIES (CPAS)

Centrum for stillahavsasienstudier
CPAS, Kraftriket, Stockholm University, SE-106 91, Sweden

tel:46-8-16-2897 fax:46-8-16-8810
e-mail:*cpas@orient.su.se*
URL:*http://www.cpas.su.se*

Organizational Status: University-affiliated institute, founded in 1984.

Background/Scope: The Center for Pacific Asia Studies (CPAS) was established to help stimulate general interest in the Asia Pacific and to give impetus and focus to academic research into regional political, economic, social and cultural developments.

Areas of Research: Foreign relations and diplomacy, security and defense, political issues, gender, intellectual history.

Geographic Focus: Global/international, especially China, Japan, Korea, Taiwan, ARF, WTO, KEDO, CSCAP, CAEC.

CENTER FOR STRATEGIC AND INTERNATIONAL STUDIES (CSIS)

1800 K Street, NW Washington, D.C. 20006, United States
tel:1-202-887-0200 fax:1-202-775-3199
e-mail:webmaster@csis.org, ehirano@csis.org
URL:http://www.csis.org

Organizational Status: Independent institute, founded in 1962.

Background/Scope: CSIS is a private, tax-exempt institution, and its research is non-partisan and non-proprietary. CSIS is a public policy research institution dedicated to policy analysis and to having an impact. CSIS is the only institution of its kind that maintains resident experts on all the world's major geographical regions. It also covers key functional areas such as international finance, emerging markets, U.S. domestic and economic policy and U.S. foreign policy and national security issues. Policy impact is the basic mission of CSIS. Its goal is to inform and shape selected policy decisions in government and the private sector to meet the increasingly complex and difficult challenges that leaders will confront in the next century.

Areas of Research: Comprehensive, with a focus on topical and regional research. The "strategic" approach of CSIS has emphasized long-range, anticipatory, and integrated thinking on a wide range of policy issues.

Geographic Focus: Domestic, global/international, especially Japan, China, Korea, India, Canada, Mexico, Russia, Africa, Asia, Caribbean, Central America, Eastern Europe, South Asia, Middle East, Eurasia, South America, Western Europe, and the Third World.

THE EDWIN O. REISCHAUER CENTER FOR EAST ASIAN STUDIES, THE PAUL H. NITZE SCHOOL OF ADVANCED INTERNATIONAL STUDIES, JOHNS HOPKINS UNIVERSITY

1619 Massachusetts Avenue, NW, Washington,
D.C. 20036, United States
tel:1-202-663-5815 fax:1-202-663-5799
e-mail:*fjshima@mail.jhuwash.jhu.edu*
URL:*http://www.sais-jhu.edu*

Organizational Status: University-affiliated institute, founded in 1984.

Background/Scope: The Reischauer Center was established in 1984 as the primary graduate institution in Washington, D.C., for training future leaders to work in U.S.–East Asian affairs. The Center is dedicated to teaching the history, culture, politics, economics and languages of Japan, China and Southeast Asia to graduate students. This is accomplished through coursework of the regions, the SAIS-Japan Forum, the SAIS-International University of Japan exchange program, summer internships and scholarships. Its mission is to continue providing resources and access to government and business leaders, scholars and journalists from East Asia.

Areas of Research: Political issues, foreign relations and diplomacy, security and defense, economic issues, industry policy, social issues.

Geographic Focus: United States, Japan, Korea.

THE HERITAGE FOUNDATION

214 Massachusetts Ave., NE, Washington,
D.C. 20002, United States
tel:1-202-546-4400 fax:1-202-546-8328
e-mail:*info@heritage.org*
URL:*http://www.heritage.org*

Organizational Status: Independent research and educational institute, founded in 1973.

Background/Scope: The foundation is a research and educational institute—a think tank—whose mission is to formulate and promote conservative public policies based on the principles of free enterprise, limited government, individual freedom, traditional American values and a strong national defense. It pursues this mission by performing timely, accurate research on key policy issues and marketing these findings effectively to its primary audiences: members of Congress, key congressional staff members, policy makers in the executive branch, the nation's news media, and the academic and policy communities. The foundation's products include publications, articles, lectures, conferences and meetings.

Areas of Research: Regional studies, industry policy, development studies, labor and human resource development, communications and information, science and technology, environment and natural resources, culture and religion, foreign relations, economic issues, social issues, health and welfare, security and defense, education, biological, agricultural and physical sciences, gender, political issues.

Geographic Focus: Domestic, international.

HOOVER INSTITUTION ON WAR, REVOLUTION AND PEACE

Hoover Institution, Stanford University, Stanford,
CA 94305-6010, United States
tel:1-650-723-0603 fax:1-650-725-8611
e-mail:*horaney@hoover.stanford.edu*
URL:*http://www-hoover.stanford.edu/*

Organizational Status: University-affiliated institute, founded in 1918.

Background/Scope: Founded as a war library by Herbert Hoover, the Institution today is a center also of scholarship and public policy research, committed to generating ideas that define a free society. The defining principles of individual, economic and political freedom, private enterprise, and representative government were fundamental to Hoover's vision. Hoover described the mission as contributing to the pursuits of securing and safeguarding peace, improving the human condition, and limiting government intrusion into the lives of individuals. This mission also is reaffirmed today.

Areas of Research: Education, political issues, foreign relations and diplomacy, economic issues, security and defense, culture and religion, environment and natural resources.

Geographic Focus: Domestic, global/international.

INSTITUTE FOR INTERNATIONAL ECONOMICS (IIE)

11 Dupont Circle, NW Suite 620,
Washington, D.C., United States
tel:1-202-328-9000 fax:1-202-328-5432
e-mail:*alreeves@iie.com*
URL:*http://www.iie.com*

Organizational Status: Independent institute, founded in 1981.

Background/Scope: The IIE is a private, non-profit, non-partisan research institution devoted to the study of international economic policy. The Institute has provided timely, objective analysis and concrete solutions to key international problems.

Areas of Research: Economic issues, industry policy, development studies, labor and human resource development, regional studies, foreign relations and diplomacy, security and defense, communications and information, environment and natural resources. IIE's focus is on areas such as: international trade, including APEC, Uruguay Round, NAFTA, and ETAA; foreign investment, including exchange rate regimes, capital flows to emerging markets, economic sanctions; international environmental policy; European Monetary Union; telecommunications; corruption; globalization; technology; unemployment; and international monetary systems, such as debt, banking issues, financial markets and crises.

Geographic Focus: Domestic, global/international, especially Japan, Korea, China, Mexico, APEC, ASEAN, Pacific Basin, Latin America, NAFTA, ETAA, EU.

INSTITUTE FOR INTERNATIONAL POLICY STUDIES (IIPS)

Sumitomo Hanzomon Bldg., 7F, 3-16 Hayabusa-cho,

Chiyoda-ku, Tokyo 102-0092, Japan
tel:81-3-3222-0711 fax:81-3-3222-0710
e-mail:*info@iips.org*
URL:*http://www.iips.org*

Organizational Status: Independent institute, founded in 1988.

Background/Scope: Established by former Prime Minister Yasuhiro Nakasone, IIPS is an independent, non-profit institution for research and study, international exchange, and other activities that contribute to a more peaceful world. IIPS, both alone and in cooperation with domestic and worldwide research organizations, examines critical issues that face the world and Japan from an independent standpoint and with a global perspective. The Institute's comprehensive approach includes politics, economics, security and the environment. It then proposes policies to address present and future global trends.

Areas of Research: Foreign relations and diplomacy, security and defense, economic issues, political issues, environment and natural resources. Current research projects are: 1) building a new framework for nuclear nonproliferation; 2) the role of a pluralistic international framework; 3) a new stage in population problems and their international implications; 4) adaptation to global standards in various fields; 5) the information era and changes in international relations; 6) environmental problems in China and Japan's response; 7) participation by Russia in a regional cooperative framework and the role of Japan; 8) toward building a new era in Japan–South Korea relations; 9) an international comparison of public welfare activities; and 10) Global Trends 2005.

Geographic Focus: Global/international.

THE INSTITUTE FOR FOREIGN POLICY ANALYSIS, INC. (IFPA)

10th Floor, 675 Massachusetts Avenue,
Cambridge, MA 02139, United States

tel:1-617-492-2116 fax:1-617-492-8242
e-mail:*mail@ifpa.org*
URL:*http://www.ifpa.org/*

Organizational Status: Independent institute, founded in 1976.

Background/Scope: The IFPA research agenda is designed to assist senior government policy makers, industry executives, technology developers, and the broader public assess the implications of the momentous shifts in global affairs that have reshaped the security landscape.

Areas of Research: Security and defense, foreign relations and diplomacy, regional studies, political issues, industry policy. IFPA's priority research areas, projects and programs include: Global Security Perspectives; The Nuclear Curriculum Working Group Project; The GCC Regional Study; Requirements for Future Missile Defense Technology Research; Missile Defense-Related Briefings; and Future Military Space Challenges.

Geographic Focus: Domestic, the countries of NATO, Europe, Baltics, Russia, China, Japan, South and North Korea, Australia, GCC nations, Canada, Western/Central/Eastern Europe, Middle East, Asia Pacific region, EU, OSCE, ASEAN.

INSTITUTE OF ASIAN AFFAIRS (IFA)

Institut fur Asienkunde
Rothenbaumchaussee 32, D-20148 Hamburg, Germany
tel:49-40-44-30-01 fax:49-40-410-79-45
e-mail: *ifahh@uni-hamburg.de* URL: *http://www.duei.de/ifa*

Organizational Status: Independent institute, founded in 1956.

Background/Scope: Established on the initiative of the German Parliament and the German Foreign Office, the Institute of Asian Affairs is an independent, non-profit organization with its own charter. The Institute has been assigned the task of studying contemporary political, economic and social developments in the Asian countries. Its work should be of practical relevance to the media, political parties, the business community and the administration.

Areas of Research: Political issues, economic issues, foreign relations and diplomacy, social issues, development studies. In addition to studies of individual Asian countries, IfA's research focuses on interregional, multinational and international relations in East and Southeast Asia; regional economic cooperation; the possibilities for economic cooperation between the Federal Republic of Germany and selected Asian countries; and political and economic turbulence in individual countries and regions of Asia and ways to overcome them.

Geographic Focus: Japan, China, Taiwan, Korea, ASEAN member countries, India, APEC, ASEM.

INSTITUTE OF POLICY STUDIES (IPS)

Victoria University of Wellington, 6 Wai-te-ata Road, Kelburn, P.O. Box 600 Wellington, New Zealand
tel:64-4-471-5307 fax:64-4-473-1261

Organizational Status: University-affiliated institute, founded in 1983.

Background/Scope: The IPS was established by Victoria University, after consultation with senior and former public sector officials, to promote study, research and discussion of current issues of public policy, both foreign and domestic. It is a link between academic research and public policy, providing independent study of issues important to New Zealand. In 1993, two semi-autonomous research centers were established within the Institute: The Health Services Research Centre, and The Centre for Strategic Studies.

Areas of Research: Economic issues, social issues, education, labor and human resource development, health and welfare, foreign relations and diplomacy. IPS's research is organized within several programs: 1) Income Distribution and Social Policy: human capital development, labor market issues, Treaty of Waitangi (domestic ethnic) issues; 2) Public Sector Management: state sector reforms, constitutional issues; 3) Business Studies and Taxation: public ownership of assets, tax systems; 4) New Zealand in the World: New Zealand's relationship with Asia.

Geographic Focus: Domestic, Asia (APEC).

INSTITUTE OF SOUTHEAST ASIAN STUDIES (ISEAS)

Heng Mui Keng Terrace, off Pasir
Panjang Road 119614, Singapore
tel:65-778-0955 fax:65-778-1735
e-mail:*chia@iseas.edu.sg*
URL:*http://www.iseas.edu.sg/*

Organizational Status: Semi-governmental institute, founded in 1968.

Background/Scope: ISEAS is a regional research institute established for scholars and other specialists concerned with modern Southeast Asia, particularly the many-faceted problems of stability and security, economic development, and political and social change. ISEAS is 30 years old, and through its various activities, has developed an extensive network of individuals and institutions worldwide. ISEAS serves as an intellectual hub and a center for the vigorous exchange of ideas, research and scholarship for both policy-relevant and contemporary issues.

Areas of Research: Regional studies, economic issues, political issues, foreign relations and diplomacy, security and defense.

Geographic Focus: ASEAN, Southeast Asia, Asia-Pacific.

INTERNATIONAL INSTITUTE FOR STRATEGIC STUDIES (IISS)

23 Tavistock Street, London WC2E 7NQ, United Kingdom
tel:44-171-379-7676 fax:44-171-836-3108
e-mail:*iiss@iiss.org.uk*
URL:*http://www.isn.ethz.ch/iiss*

Organizational Status: Independent institute, founded in 1958.

Background/Scope: IISS is an independent center for research, information, and debate on the modern world. The aims of the Institute are as follows: 1) to provide a firm foundation of accurate information on and rigorous analysis of current and future problems, and to assist the public comprehension of key international security and strategic issues; and 2) to promote professional debate and scholarship in international security matters by providing a forum for the exchange of views and facilities for members.

Areas of Research: Foreign relations and diplomacy, security and defense, regional studies.

Geographic Focus: Global/international.

KOREA DEVELOPMENT INSTITUTE (KDI)

207-41 Chongnyangni-dong, Tongdaemun-gu,
P.O. Box 113, Chongnyang Seoul 130-010, Korea
tel:82-2-958-4114 fax:82-2-961-5092
e-mail:*presdnt@kdiux.kdi.re.kr*

Organizational Status: Semi-governmental institute, founded in 1971.

Background/Scope: The KDI is an autonomous, policy-oriented research organization. KDI was established by the Korean government as an economic think tank to provide a rigorous academic perspective on the various economic policy issues that had arisen during Korea's rapid growth and development in the 1960s. Since then, the scope of KDI's activities has grown, and it is now called upon to provide expert analysis and advice on all aspects of long- and short-term government policies in areas ranging from domestic economic policy to international trade and investment. In addition, KDI has played an increasingly important role in promoting international economic cooperation. By sponsoring international forums on development and maintaining close links with research organizations and individual scholars all over the globe, KDI helps to strengthen ties between Korea and the rest of the world. KDI has established the KDI School of International Policy and Management in 1997 to meet the educational needs for improved policy-making and management in today's globalizing economy.

Areas of Research: Economic issues, industry policy, regional studies, health and welfare, environment and natural resources.

Geographic Focus: Domestic, global/international, with a particular interest in North Korean economy.

KOREA INSTITUTE FOR DEFENSE ANALYSES (KIDA)

Chung Ryang P.O. Box 250, Seoul 130-650, Korea
tel:82-2-961-1652 fax:82-2-965-3295
e-mail:*kjda@home.kida.re.kr*

Organizational Status: Independent institute, founded in 1979.

Background/Scope: KIDA was founded as an organization affiliated with the Agency for Defense Development (ADD) to provide the ROK Ministry of National Defense (MND) with policy alternatives. The Institute separated from the ADD and became an autonomous, non-profit research organization, fully sponsored by the government in 1987. The Institute is devoted to research on strategic environment, security policy, national defense strategy, force development, manpower management, defense economy, weapon systems acquisition policy, defense automation and arms control.

Areas of Research: Security and defense, foreign relations and diplomacy. The Institute is currently paying special attention to war game model development, which is aimed at developing a combat model appropriate to the Korean terrain and situation.

Geographic Focus: Domestic, global/international, particularly Northeast Asia.

KOREA INSTITUTE FOR INDUSTRIAL ECONOMICS AND TRADE (KIET)

Cheongryang, P.O. Box 205, Seoul, Korea
tel:82-2-962-6211 fax:82-2-963-8540/969-8540
e-mail:*oyahn@kiet.re.kr*
URL:*http://www.kiet.re.kr*

Organizational Status: Semi-governmental institute, founded in 1976.

Background/Scope: The KIET is an autonomous economic research institute established by the Korean government. KIET acts as an economic think tank analyzing economic trends, advising the Korean government on industrial, trade and commercial policies, and researching effective strategies for the public and the private sectors to increase national productivity, efficiency and competitiveness. KIET's major research activities cover the analysis and forecasting of industrial and economic trends, with a focus on identifying and exploring the ways and means to strengthen economic efficiency and industrial competitiveness. KIET recently extended and enhanced the scope of its work to include business consulting in order to further assist the industrial sector.

Areas of Research: KIET's priority research areas include: knowledge-based industry studies; industrial policy studies; small and venture business studies; distribution and regional industry studies; digital economy studies; industrial cooperation studies; and economic surveys and forecasting.

Geographic Focus: Domestic, global/international.

KOREA INSTITUTE FOR INTERNATIONAL ECONOMICS POLICY (KIEP)

300-4 Yomgok-dong, Seocho-gu, Seoul 137-747, South Korea
tel: 82-2 3460 1001 fax: 82-2 3460 1199
e-mail: *webadmin@kiep.go.kr* URL: *http://www.kiep.go.kr*

Organizational Status: Governmental institute, founded in 1989.

Background/Scope: KIEP, founded as an economic research institute, is an institute on the international economy and its relationship with Korea. It advises the national government on all major international economic policy issues and serves as a warehouse of information on Korean government policies pertaining to international economics. In addition, the institute carries out research projects for foreign institutes and governments on all areas of the Korean and international economies. Through its research, KIEP aims to : 1) Examine international factors that threaten economic stability and develop appropriate countermeasures; 2) Develop trade policies aimed at increasing exports and expanding import liberalization; 3) Develop reform measures to attract foreign direct investment, and refine corporate structures and expand overseas direct investment (ODI) to help Korean businesses enhance their presence in the world economy; and 4) Analyze the economic trends of major countries and regions.

Areas of Research: Global economic trends, exchange rate policies, international monetary and financial cooperation, world trade structures and multilateral trade organizations (WTO, OCED, APEC), commercial policies, trade disputes, economic and corporate reform.

Geographic Focus: Domestic, international.

KOREA INSTITUTE FOR
NATIONAL UNIFICATION (KINU)

SL Tobong P.O. Box 22, Seoul 142-600, Korea
tel:82-2-900-4300 fax:82-2-901-2541
e-mail:*kinu@ku.kinu.or.kr*

Organizational Status: Semi-governmental institute, founded in 1991.

Background/Scope: KINU is a nonprofit organization devoted to studies on issues related to the unification of the Korean Peninsula and to supporting the formulation of unification policy options for the government of the Republic of Korea. KINU was established to help the nation meet various crucial challenges arising from rapid changes in the global scene.

Areas of Research: Political issues, security and defense, foreign relations and diplomacy, regional studies. The Division of North Korean Political & Military Studies collects basic information and data and will publish a theoretical textbook on North Korean studies. In addition, to help the government shape policies on North Korea and unification, KINU surveys public opinion on unification issues. The Division of North Korean Social & Economic Studies studies trends of social and economic changes in North Korea. The Division of International Studies develops a formula for building a peace system on the Korean peninsula and a measure for creating a favorable environment for Korean unification through studies on the Northeast Asian situation and on Korea's relationship with its four neighboring countries. The Division of Unification Policy studies the implementation of the Basic Agreement and develops a formula for building a peace system on the Korean peninsula. KINU will also study methods for the successful operation of the KEDO project.

Geographic Focus: Domestic, global/international, particularly North Korea and Northeast Asia.

THE KOREAN INSTITUTE OF INTERNATIONAL STUDIES (KIIS)

Yongsan-ku Hangang-ro 3 ka 63-70, Dongjo
Building 4th Floor, Seoul, Korea 140-013
K.P.O Box 426, Seoul 110-604, Korea
tel:82-2-3785-2567/8 fax:82-2-3785-3453/4
e-mail:*kiiss@chollian.net*

Organizational Status: Independent institute, founded in 1965.

Background/Scope: KIIS was founded as a research institute and think tank to provide theoretical and practical foundations for the promotion of international cooperation and relations. Since 1970, in addition to covering the major powers in the international community, KIIS has extended its sphere of interest to other countries, those which had no diplomatic relations with Korea. As a result of constant efforts, KIIS could thereby facilitate the establishment of diplomatic relations with China, the Soviet Union, and East European countries. To attain this purpose, KIIS has not only sponsored dozens of annual international conferences focusing on timely topics of international relations, but it began to host bilateral roundtable conferences with both China and Russia several times a year in conjunction with many other foreign institutes. Presently the Institute's research interests lie primarily in the following areas: 1) Korea–U.S., Korea–China, and Korea–Russia relations; 2) Korea–Japan relations and Japan's post–Cold War role in the Asia-Pacific; 3) international security and arms control; 4) East Asian regional politics; and 5) environmental issues, particularly in the Far East.

Areas of Research: Foreign relations and diplomacy, security and defense, economic issues, regional studies.

Geographic Focus: U.S.A, China, Japan, Russia, North Korea, Eastern European countries, Northeast Asia, ASEAN.

THE SEJONG INSTITUTE

230 Shiheung-dong, Sujong-gu Sungnam-shi, Kyonggi-do, 461-370, Korea tel:82-2-233-9351 fax:82-2-233-8832

Organizational Status: Independent institute, registered as a non-profit legal entity with the Ministry of Foreign Affairs and Trade, founded in 1986.

Background/Scope: The Sejong Institute undertakes social science-oriented research on Korea's national security, unification, and external relations. The institute also makes policy recommendations to appropriate government agencies whenever such needs arise.

Areas of Research: Foreign relations and diplomacy, security and defense, North Korea, inter–Korean relations, regional studies.

Geographic Focus: Domestic, North Korea.

WEATHERHEAD CENTER FOR INTERNATIONAL AFFAIRS, HARVARD UNIVERSITY (WCFIA)

Harvard University, 1737 Cambridge Street, Cambridge, MA 02138, United States tel:1-617-495-4420 fax:1-617-495-8292 URL:*http://data.fas.harvard.edu/cfia/index.htm*

Organizational Status: University-affiliated institute, founded in 1958.

Background/Scope: The Center provides a multidisciplinary environment for policy-relevant research on international issues that is both academically rigorous and tied to contemporary policies and problems. The Weatherhead Center is structured to encourage the highest practical level of personal and intellectual interaction among a diverse community of scholars and practitioners. It is distinctive in its recognition that knowledge is not only a product of individual academic research, but also of vigorous, sustained intellectual dialogue among scholars and nonacademic experts. To stimulate this dialogue, the Weatherhead Center sponsors a wide array of seminars, research programs, workshops, and conferences. These activities not only encourage interaction among resident affiliates, but also serve to involve a wide variety of scholars, government officials, representatives of the private sector, and others from around the world.

Areas of Research: Political issues, foreign relations and diplomacy, security and defense, economic issues, industry policy, development studies, regional studies, social issues.

Geographic Focus: Global/international.

Index

account deficits 172
Acheson, Dean 10, 42
Advanced country 102
Afghanistan 7, 147, 155; children 138
Agreed Framework 16–17, 63, 83, 99
Al Qaeda 173
Albright, Madeleine 90
Amoco 120
Another Japan 46
Antiballistic Missile Treaty 173
Armistice Agreement (1953) 11, 37, 43
Asian Development Bank 155
Asian financial crisis 106
AT&T 121
Aurora Partners 117
Autarkic system 86, 107
Axis of evil 7, 12, 30, 47, 90, 154

Ballistic missiles 92
Bangladesh 138
Bank of Korea 24, 80, 81
Berlin Declaration 22
Berlin Free University 22

Berlin Wall 21
Biological Weapons Convention 173
Boeing 119
British Petroleum 120
Budget deficit 172
Bureaucratic organization 125
Bush, George W. 30, 47, 63–64, 90, 156, 173
Business-government cooperation 125

Cairo Conference 40
Carter, Ashton 169
Carter, Jimmy 16
Center for Arms Control and Non-Proliferation 167
Centrally planned economy 66
Checkbook diplomacy 85
China 68, 172
Chinese herbs 138
Choson dynasty 14
Choson Kingdom 38
Christian Association for Medical Mission (CAMM) 142–144

217

Clinton, Bill 16, 37, 156
Coca-Cola 118
Cold War 21
Commando forces 64
Comprehensive Test Ban Treaty 173
Confucianism 46, 47, 52–54, 68–69
Construction of new plants (internal growth) 119
Contract manufacturing 122
Contractual Joint Venture Law 87, 88
Council of Private Organizations 136
Cuba 80, 130, 155

Demilitarized zone (DMZ) 11, 37
Democratic People's Republic of Korea 9
Dunkin Donuts 122

East Europe 21
East Germany 52
Eastern decorum 53
Economic climate 129
Economic reform 69–70
Enforcement Decree of Foreign Investment Protection Act 107–108
Equity alliances 121, 123
Ethiopian famine 79
Eurasian markets 118
European Union 91, 172
Exogenous economic shocks 65–66
Exports 119
Expropriation of alien assets 129

Famine 157–158
Fast-food operations 122
First-strike doctrine 167
Food shortages 66
Foreign Enterprises Law 87, 88
Foreign direct investment, benefits of 117
Foreign entry modes 119–122
Foreign Equity Law 87
Foreign relations 129

Foreign Relations Committee 169
Foreign Trade Act of 2001 107
Four Pacific powers 12, 47, 90, 156
Four party talks 18
Franchisers 122
Franchising agreement 121
Free Economic and Trade Zone 87, 123
Friendly prices 25

General Electric 119
General Mills 120
General Motors 119
Germany 51, 69
Global economy 125
Greater China 171
Gross national product (GNP) 12, 101

Hawks 165
Hay, Michael 125
Heavy industry 102
Hermit Kingdom 38
Hilton 122
Humanitarian Code of Conduct 147
Hyundai Group of South Korea 82

IBM 119, 121
ICBM 18
Imperial Prescript of 1910 38
Inchon 10
Independent states 21
India 138
Industrial capital stock 78
Industrialized country 46
Infrastructure 38
Inner-directed economy 29, 79
Intangible benefits of foreign direct investment 117
Inter-Korean economic cooperation 83–86
Inter-Korean economic relations 99–112
Inter-Korean investment 107–108
Inter-Korean trade 105–106
International Atomic Energy Agency (IAEA) 15

International Criminal Court 173
International Federation of Red
  Cross 139
International Monetary Fund 155
International NGOs 147
Iraq 155, 172, 174
Isaacs, John 167

Japan: emperor 38; management
  style 124–126
Joint ventures 120, 123
Juche 12–15, 46, 55–57, 69, 86,
  107; farming 14, 56
June 2000 summit talks 23
Jung Ju Young 148

Kaesong City 23, 85
Kaesong ginseng 129
Kelly, James 18, 91
Kelly Services 122
Kim Dae Jung 22, 83–86, 141
Kim Hyung Suk 135, 144–146
Kim Il Sung 9, 12, 41–42
Kim Jong Il 12, 54, 164
Korea 69; division of 40–41; gov-
  ernment 38; humanitarian assis-
  tance 140–141; NGOs 135–149;
  peninsula 38; unifications 61–71
Korean Christian Association 140
Korean Communist Party 42
Korean Energy Development Cor-
  poration (KEDO) 17, 91
Korean Food for the Hungary
  International 144
Korean Foundation for World Aid
  138, 144–146
Korean War 10–12, 37–47; conse-
  quences of 44–47
Korean Workers Party 12
Korean Youth Association 138
Koryo hotel 128
Kyoto Protocol 173

Land of Morning Calm 38
Law on Cooperative Exchange be-
  tween North and South Korea 136
Libya 155
Licensing agreement 121

Lifetime employment 125
Light industry 102
Light water reactors (LWR) 17
Little Japan 46
Location marketing 111
"Loving Rice" 140
Lugar, Richard 169

MacArthur, Douglas 43
Magnesia 117
Mandate of Heaven 38
Maquiladoras 117–118
March First Independence Move-
  ment 38
Market economy 148
Market oriented economic reform
  70
Market price 104
Marketing, concept of 110–111
Marxist-Leninist principles 12
McDonald's 122
Medical Supply for Children 138
Mergers and acquisitions (external
  growth) 120
Military Armistice Commission
  (MAC) 11, 44
Missile defense systems 18
Multilateralism 173
Multinational companies 118
Multiple entry modes 123

National Press Club 10, 42
Natsios, Andrew S. 80
Natural laws of politics 61
Natural resources, undevloped 116,
  117, 130
Nestlé of Switzerland 120
Neutral Nations Supervisory Com-
  mission (NSC) 11, 44
New York Times 159
Next Japan 46
Nixon, Richard 171
Nobel Peace Prize 16, 23
Nonaggression pact 91
Non-commercial transactions 105
Non-economic incentives 24
Non-government organizations
  (NGOs) 136

North Korea 8, 29, 174; collapse of 65–67; domestic dilemmas 62; economy 23–26, 77–93; famine 179–82, 35–149; future of 26–29; health care 138; legal system 86–89; nuclear weapons program 15–20; per capita income 101; military capabilities 64
Nuclear Non-Proliferation Treaty (NPT) 15, 19

Obstacles to foreign investment 130
Official government price 104
OPEC oil embargo 172
Open-door policy 107, 108
Open economy 88
Operational restrictions 129
Organization for Economic Cooperation and Development (OECD) 46

Pacific powers *see* Four Pacific powers
Pagoda Park 39
Panmunjom 44
Paris Peace Conference 38
Park, Thomas 135
Partnerships 123
Peace and prosperity 170
Perry, William 89, 156, 167
Perry process 89, 156
Political climate 129
Political risks 129; analysis 129–131
Poverty trap 70
Powell, Colin 90
Powell, John 138
Primary products 105
Processing-on-commission 84, 118
Product marketing 111
Pusan 10
Pyongyang 44

Quasi-barter system 25, 81

Rations 104, 163
Respiratory diseases 139
Rhee, Syngman 42

Right of self-determination 38
Rogue states 80
Roh Moo Hyun 92, 169–170
Russia 147; revolution 80

Self-reliance 12–15, 54–57, 68–69
Seoul 10, 27
September 11, 2001, terrorist attacks 7
Sino-Soviet treaty *see* Treaty of Friendship, Alliance, and Mutual Assistance
Socialist constitution 12, 87
Socialist-friendly prices 81
South Africa 155
South Korea 8, 43, 68; economy 102; government 146; per capita income 101; Workers' Party 42
Soviet Union 21, 40, 102, 171
Special Administrative Area 87, 123
Spiral of expectations 92
Sputnik 171
Stalin, Joseph 44, 47
Strategic distribution location 118
Strategic role 117
Sunshine policy 22–26, 83–86, 141
Syria 130

Taliban 7
Technical state of war 11
Third People's Hospital (Pyongyang) 141, 143
Third World countries 142
The 38th parallel 9, 40, 41, 44
Trade imbalance between two Koreas 106
Transparency of distribution 137
Treaty of Friendship, Alliance, and Mutual Assistance 11, 45
Truman, Harry S 10, 43
Two-Korea policy 15
Two-stage missile 17
Two-state peninsula 66–67
Two-tier pricing levels 104
Types of political risks 129

Unilateralism 171
United Nations (UN) 9, 41

UN Commission on Korea (UNCK) 9, 41
UN Security Council 43
United States: decline 171–174; economic sanctions 155; hegemony 174; legal sanctions 83, 156; management style 124–126; Pediatric Society 139; U.S. Security Council 18
U.S. Pediatric Society 139
U.S.-Soviet Joint Commission 9, 41
Uzbekistan 147

Vaccines 138
Vietnam War 172
Vitamin A 139
War economics 65

Warlords of factions 169
Watergate scandal 172
Wholly owned subsidiaries 123
Wilson, Woodrow 38
Work ethics 125
World Bank 155
World Food Program (WFP) 79, 137, 157
World Health Organization (WHO) 138
World Medical Relief 144
World War II 9, 40

Yalta Agreement 40
Yalu River 44
Yangban class 38
Yanggakdo hotel 128
Yongbyon site 15